W9-AEJ-104

Sadlier

WE·BELIEVE ™

We Are the Church

WITH PROJECT DISCIPLE
Pray
Learn
Celebrate
Share
Choose
Live

Grade Three

Sadlier

Nihil Obstat
Monsignor Michael F. Hull, S.T.D.
Censor Librorum

Imprimatur
✠ Most Reverend Dennis J. Sullivan, D.D.
Vicar General of the Archdiocese of New York
January 27, 2010

The *Nihil Obstat* and *Imprimatur* are official declaration that these books are free of doctrinal or moral error. No implications contained therein that those who have granted the *Nihil Obstat* and *Imprimatur* agree with the content, opinion or statements expressed.

Acknowledgments

Excerpts from the English translation of *The Roman Missal*, © 2010, International Committee on English in the Liturgy, Inc. All rights reserved.

Excerpts from the English translation of the *Catechism of the Catholic Church* for the United States of America, copyright © 1994, United States Catholic Conference, Inc.—Libreria Editrice Vaticana. English translation of the *Catechism of the Catholic Church: Modifications from the Editio Typica* copyright © 1997, United States Catholic Conference, Inc.—Libreria Editrice Vaticana. Used with permission.

Scripture excerpts are taken from the *New American Bible with Revised New Testament and Psalms.* Copyright © 1991, 1986, 1970 Confraternity of Christian Doctrine, Inc., Washington, DC. Used with permission. All rights reserved. No part of the *New American Bible* may be reproduced by any means without permission in writing from the copyright owner.

Excerpts from the English translation of *Lectionary for Mass* © 1969, 1981, ICEL; excerpts from the English translation of *Rite of Holy Week* © 1972, ICEL; excerpts from the English translation of the *Rite of Penance* © 1974, ICEL; excerpts from the English translation of *Eucharistic Prayers for Masses of Reconciliation* © 1975, ICEL; excerpts from the English translation of *Pastoral Care of the Sick: Rites of Anointing and Viaticum* © 1982, ICEL; excerpts from the English translation of *A Book of Prayers* © 1982, ICEL; All rights reserved.

Excerpts from *Catholic Household Blessings and Prayers* Copyright © 1988 United States Catholic Conference, Inc. Washington, DC. Used with permission. All rights reserved.

English translation of the Lord's Prayer, Glory Be to the Father, and the Apostles' Creed by the International Consultation on English Texts. (ICET)

"We Believe, We Believe in God," © 1979, North American Liturgy Resources (NALR), 5536 NE Hassalo, Portland, OR 97213. All rights reserved. Used with permission. "Lift High the Cross," words: George W. Kitchin; rev. Michael R. Newbolt. © 1974 by Hope Publishing Co.,

Carol Stream, IL 60188. All rights reserved. Used with permission. "Whatsoever You Do," © 1966, 1982, Willard F. Jabusch. Administered by OCP Publications, 5536 NE Hassalo, Portland, OR 97213. All rights reserved. Used with permission. "Jesus Is with Us," © 1990, OCP Publications, 5536 NE Hassalo, Portland, OR 97213. All rights reserved. Used with permission. "We Sing Your Glory," © 1999, Bernadette Farrell. Published by OCP Publications, 5536 NE Hassalo, Portland, OR 97213. All rights reserved. Used with permission. "They'll Know We Are Christians," Peter Scholtes. © 1966, F.E.L. Publications, Ltd., assigned 1991 to the Lorenz Corporation. All rights reserved. International copyright secured. Used with permission. "Only a Shadow," © 1971, Carey Landry and North American Liturgy Resources (NALR), 5536 NE Hassalo, Portland, OR 97213. All rights reserved. Used with permission. "Prepare the Way," © 1991, Christopher Walker. Published by OCP Publications, 5536 NE Hassalo, Portland, OR 97213. All rights reserved. Used with permission. "Do Not Delay," © 1995, Anne Quigley. Published by OCP Publications, 5536 NE Hassalo, Portland, OR 97213. All rights reserved. Used with permission. "Jesus, We Believe in You," © 1990, Carey Landry and North American Liturgy Resources (NALR), 5536 NE Hassalo, Portland, OR 97213. All rights reserved. Used with permission. "Walking Up to Jesus," © 1993, Daughters of Charity and Christopher Walker. Published by OCP Publications, 5536 NE Hassalo, Portland, OR 97213. All rights reserved. Used with permission. "Ashes," © 1978, New Dawn Music, 5536 NE Hassalo, Portland, OR 97213. All rights reserved. Used with permission. "We Are the Church," © 1991, Christopher Walker. Published by OCP Publications, 5536 NE Hassalo, Portland, OR 97213. All rights reserved. Used with permission. "We Are the Church" was originally from "Come, Follow Me" music program, Benziger Publishing Company. "Sing a Song to the Saints," © 1991, Jack Louden. Published by OCP Publications, 5536 NE Hassalo, Portland, OR 97213. All rights reserved. Used with permission. "Glory and Praise to Our God," © 1976, Daniel L. Schutte and New Dawn Music, 5536 NE Hassalo, Portland, OR 97213. All rights reserved. Used with permission.

Copyright © 2011 by William H. Sadlier, Inc. All rights reserved. This book, or any part thereof, may not be reproduced in any form, or by any means, including electronic, photographic, or mechanical, or by any sound recording system, or by any device for storage and retrieval of information, without the written permission of the publisher.

Printed in the United States of America.

S® is a registered trademark of William H. Sadlier, Inc.
We Believe™ is a registered trademark of William H. Sadlier, Inc.

William H. Sadlier, Inc.
9 Pine Street
New York, NY 10005-4700

ISBN: 978-0-8215-6403-5
7 8 9 10 WEBC 16 15 14

The Subcommittee on the Catechism, United States Conference of Catholic Bishops, has found this catechetical series, copyright 2011, to be in conformity with the *Catechism of the Catholic Church*.

Photo Credits

Cover Photography: Alamy/Photodisc/Amos Morgan: *blond girl*; Ken Karp: *boy and girl*; Photolibrary/Ken Wardius: *hand with seedling*; Punchstock/Photodisc: *bird bath, park*. Interior: age fotostock/Corbis RF/Randy Faris: 224. Alamy/Blend Images: 18 *top*; Israel Images: 32; Jim Corwin: 96; Mode Images Limited: 186; Photo Alto: 169 *bottom*; Pontino: 182; Phil Seale: 136; Stockbyte: 225; Tetra Images: 240. Animals Animals/Earth Scenes/John Gerlach: 94 *top*. AP Photo/Steve Ruark: 15, 89. Art Resource, NY/Bridgeman-Giraudon: 222; Scala: 18 *bottom*, 55, 212 *top*, 247. Dave Bartuff: 121. Lori Berkowitz: 206 *bottom*. Jane Bernard: 3, 68 *bottom*, 73 *center right*, 100 *top*, 104 *right*, 129, 142, 148 *bottom*, 149, 150, 158, 159, 171, 173 *top*, 184, 206 *top*, 223 *top*, 242. Bob Daemmrich Photo, Inc.: 174 *left*. Bridge Building Images/Fr. John Guiliani: 213. The Bridgeman Art Library/Museo de Santa Cruz, Toledo, Spain: 44; Sant'Apollinare Nuovo, Ravenna, Italy/Lauros/Giraudon: 253. Karen Callaway: 17 *left*, 59 *bottom*, 60 *bottom*, 65, 73 *right*, 102 *right*, 133, 143, 144, 173 *bottom*, 174 *right*, 179 *top*, 190 *top*, 230. Catholic Relief Services/Operation Rice Bowl: 174 *bottom*. Corbis/Ed Bock: 29 *top right*; Bowers Museum of Cultural Art, Santa Ana, CA: 212 *bottom*; Owen Franken: 92 *center*; Julie Habel: 185 *center*, 212 *bottom*; Lindsay Hebberd: 196 *top left*; KIPA/Sergio Gaudenti: 92 *bottom right*, 243 *left*; David Lees: 86 *top*; Lawrence Manning: 10 *bottom*, 109; Mug Shots: 111 *top*; Ariel Skelley: 59 *center*; Joseph Sohm: 108 *center*; Tom Stewart: 108 *bottom*; Sygma/Caron Philippe: 198–199; Peter Turnley: 196 *center*. The Crosiers/Gene Plaisted, OSC: 68 *top*, 118, 120, 122, 140–141, 161 *top*, 169 *top*, 179 *bottom*, 248. Used with permission from Diocese of Cleveland/University of Mary Washington, Fredericksburg, VA Yearbook 1973: *Jean Donovan* 137 *bottom right*. Dreamstime.com/Elena Elisseeva: 152 *bottom*. Neal Farris: 10 *top*, 11, 12 *bottom*, 14 *top*, 27, 38 *bottom*, 73 *center left*, 75, 78–79, 91, 95, 101 *bottom*, 102 *bottom left*, 110, 115, 116, 117, 123, 147, 227, 232, 241 *left*, 243 *right*. Getty Images/AFP: 86 *bottom*, 161 *bottom*; AFP/Gabriel Bouys: 74; Blend Images/Jose Luis Pelaez Inc.: 16 *top*; Digital Vision: 219 *background*; Eyewire: 108 *top left*, 155 *clock illustration*; Getty Images News/William Thomas Cain: 152 *top*; The Image Bank/Terry Donnelly: 107 *background*; The Image Bank/Ross M. Horowitz: 94–95 *background*; The Image Bank/David Zelick: 302 *center*; Photodisc: 11 *bottom right*, 29, 64 *top*, 85, 94–95, 131 *left*, 206–207; Stockbyte: 196–197; Stone/Leland Bobbe: 197 *bottom*; Stone/Daniel Bosler: 94 *bottom*; Stone/Paul Chesley: 197 *top*; Stone/John Lawrence: 201 *top*; Stone/Silvestre Machado: 87 *top*; Stone/Will & Deni McIntyre: 66 *top*; Stone/Lori Adamski Peek: 73 *center*, 84 *center*; Stone/Don Smetzer: 66 *bottom*; Stone/Terry Vine: 185 *center right*; Stone/Stuart Westmorland: 209 *bottom*; Taxi/Charles Benes: 131 *background*; Taxi/Patrick Molnar: 191 *top*; Time & Life Pictures/Robert Nicklesberg: 92 *top*; Time & Life Pictures/Ben Van Hook: 93 *bottom*. Anne Hamersky: 97. © 2008 Michael Hudson, All Rights Reserved. Stock usage permission granted for Catholic Health Association and Provena Health: 168. The Image Works/Bob Daemmrich: 87 *bottom*; Journal Courier/Steve Warmowski: 37 *bottom*. Ken Karp: 12 *top*, 13 *top*, 14 *bottom*, 16 *bottom*, 17 *center left*, 17 *right*, 19, 30 *bottom*, 35, 43, 51, 59 *top*, 83, 99, 102 *top left*, 107, 131, 139 *top center*, 139 *bottom*, 139 *top left*, 155, 172, 185 *center left*, 187, 190 *bottom*, 195, 211, 215, 216, 219, 221, 237, 250, 252. Sister Jane Keegan: 38 *top*, 251. The Kobal Collection/New Line/Jaimie Trueblood: 217. Greg Lord: 13 *bottom*, 134 *bottom*, 163, 165 *center*, 203, 214, 241 *right*. Maryknoll Mission Archive: *Sister Maura Clarke* 137 *top right*, *Sister Ita Ford* 137 *top left*. Norton Simon Art Foundation/Gift of Mr. Norton Simon, 1976, Pasadena, CA: 30 *top*. Natural Selection Stock Photography/Black Sheep/Kazuyoshi Onishi: 166–167. Karin Anderson-Pauzar: 207 *top*. PhotoEdit, Inc./Tom Carter: 167; Myrleen Pearson: 185 *right*, 223 *bottom*; James Shaffer: 166. Photolibrary/age fotostock/Terrance Klassen: 105; James Frank: 139 *top right*; Imagestate Pictor: 204 *top*, 205 *top*. Punchstock/Corbis: 209 *top*; Photodisc: 200; PictureIndia: 112. Reuters/Jayanta Shaw: 196 *bottom*. Aaron Rosenberg: 132. Deacon Thomas Stadnik: 205 *bottom*. Chris Sheridan: 2, 78, 84 *top*, 84 *bottom*, 101 *top*, 204 *bottom*. SuperStock/Francisco Cruz: 29 *center right*; Lisette Le Bon: 60 *top*. Lu Taskey: 207 *bottom*. Used with permission from Ursuline Sisters of Cleveland: *Sister Dorothy Kazel* 137 *bottom left*. W.P. Wittman Ltd: 93 *top*, 134 *top*, 145, 148 *top*, 151, 165 *top*, 176, 177, 178, 180, 244. Wikimedia Commons: 145.

Illustrator Credits

Series Patterned Background Design: Evan Polenghi. Bernard Adnet: 163. Jo Lynn Alcorn: 211, 214–215. Bassino & Guy: 24, 40, 48, 49. Teresa Berasi: 46–47. Don Bishop: 102, 103. Ken Bowser: 155. Carly Castillon: 139. Anne Cook: 99. Laura DeSantis: 78–79. Mena Dolobowsky: 25, 160 *top*. Nancy Doniger: 38–39. Patrick Faricy: 6, 17 *insets*, 20, 21, 22, 23, 28, 31, 36–37, 54, 68–69 *insets*, 73 *inset*, 76–77, 129 *inset left*, 130, 156–157, 164, 188–189, 228–229, 245. Mary Haverfield: 150–151. Donna Ingemanson: 75. W. B. Johnston: 100–101, 164–165 *background*, 232. Ken Joudrey: 220–221, 252. David Scott Meier: 187. Cheryl Mendenhall: 185 *inset*. Bob Ostrom: 15, 41, 56, 57, 80, 89, 160 *bottom*, 192, 193, 217. Gary Phillips: 238–239. Mark Radencich: 44–45. Ursula Roma: 59, 60–61, 62–63, 65, 66–67, 68, 69, 70, 115, 116–117, 118–119, 121, 122–123, 124, 125, 171, 172–173, 174, 175, 176, 177, 178–179, 180, 181, 182, 227, 228–229 *top border*, 230–231. Nigel Sandor: 110–111. Stacey Schuett: 129 *inset right*. Jane Shasky: 68–69 *map*. Victor Shatunov: 92–93. Susan Swan: 19. Kat Thacker: 148–149. Tom White: 108–109. Ann Wilson: 113. Nicholas Wilton: 222–223. Amy Wummer: 33, 97, 145, 201.

The Sadlier *We Believe* Program was drawn from the wisdom of the community. It was developed by nationally recognized experts in catechesis, curriculum, and child development. These teachers of the faith and practitioners helped us to frame every lesson to be age-appropriate and appealing. In addition, a team including respected catechetical, liturgical, pastoral, and theological experts shared their insights and inspired the development of the program.

Contributors to the inspiration and development are:

Dr. Gerard F. Baumbach
Director, Center for Catechetical Initiatives
Concurrent Professor of Theology
University of Notre Dame
Notre Dame, Indiana

Carole M. Eipers, D.Min.
Vice President, Executive Director
    of Catechetics
William H. Sadlier, Inc.

Catechetical and Liturgical Consultants

Patricia Andrews
Director of Religious Education
Our Lady of Lourdes Church,
Slidell, LA

Reverend Monsignor John F. Barry, P.A.
Pastor, American Martyrs Parish
Manhattan Beach, CA

Mary Jo Tully
Chancellor, Archdiocese of Portland

Reverend Monsignor John M. Unger
Deputy Superintendent for Catechesis
    and Evangelization
Archdiocese of St. Louis

Curriculum and Child Development Consultants

Brother Robert R. Bimonte, FSC
Executive Director
NCEA Department of Elementary Schools

Sr. Carol Cimino, SSJ, Ed.D.
National Consultant
William H. Sadlier

Gini Shimabukuro, Ed.D.
Associate Professor
Catholic Educational Leadership Program
School of Education
University of San Francisco

Catholic Social Teaching Consultants

John Carr
Executive Director
Department of Justice, Peace,
    and Human Development
United States Conference of Catholic Bishops
Washington, D.C.

Joan Rosenhauer
Associate Director
Department of Justice, Peace,
    and Human Development
United States Conference of Catholic Bishops
Washington, D.C.

Inculturation Consultants

Allan Figueroa Deck, S.J., Ph.D., S.T.D.
Executive Director
Secretariat of Cultural Diversity in the Church
United States Conference of Catholic Bishops
Washington, D.C.

Kirk P. Gaddy, Ed.D.
Educational Consultant
Baltimore, MD

Reverend Nguyễn Việt Hưng
Vietnamese Catechetical Committee

Dulce M. Jiménez-Abreu
Director of Bilingual Programs
William H. Sadlier, Inc.

Scriptural Consultant

Reverend Donald Senior, CP, Ph.D., S.T.D.
Member, Pontifical Biblical Commission
President, The Catholic Theological Union
Chicago, IL

Theological Consultants

Most Reverend Edward K. Braxton, Ph.D., S.T.D.
Official Theological Consultant
Bishop of Belleville

Norman F. Josaitis, S.T.D.
Theological Consultant

Reverend Joseph A. Komonchak, Ph.D.
Professor, School of Theology and Religious Studies
The Catholic University of America

Most Reverend Richard J. Malone, Th.D.
Bishop of Portland, ME

Sister Maureen Sullivan, OP, Ph.D.
Associate Professor
St. Anselm College
Manchester, NH

Mariology Consultant

Sister M. Jean Frisk, ISSM, S.T.L.
International Marian Research Institute
Dayton, OH

Media/Technology Consultants

Sister Judith Dieterle, SSL
Past President, National Association of
Catechetical Media Professionals

Sister Jane Keegan, RDC
Technology Consultant

Michael Ferejohn
Director of Electronic Media
William H. Sadlier, Inc.

Robert T. Carson
Electronic Media Design Director
William H. Sadlier, Inc.

Erik Bowie
Electronic Media Production Manager
William H. Sadlier, Inc.

Writing/Development Team

Rosemary K. Calicchio
Vice President, Publications

Blake Bergen
Editorial Director

Melissa D. Gibbons
Director of Research and
Development

MaryAnn Trevaskiss
Supervising Editor

Maureen Gallo
Senior Editor, Project Director

Christian Garcia
Contributing Writer

Kathy Hendricks
Contributing Writer

Joanne McDonald
Senior Editor

Allison Johnston
Senior Editor

William M. Ippolito
Executive Consultant

Margherita Rotondi
Editorial Assistant

Sadlier Consulting Team

Michaela Burke Barry
Director of Consultant Services

Judith A. Devine
National Sales Consultant

Kenneth Doran
National Religion Consultant

Saundra Kennedy, Ed.D.
National Religion Consultant

Victor Valenzuela
National Religion Consultant

Publishing Operations Team

Deborah Jones
Vice President,
Publishing Operations

Vince Gallo
Creative Director

Francesca O'Malley
Associate Art Director

Jim Saylor
Photography Manager

Design/Photo Staff
Andrea Brown, Kevin Butler,
Debrah Kaiser, Susan Ligertwood,
Cesar Llacuna, Bob Schatz

Production Staff
Diane Ali, Monica Bernier,
Barbara Brown, Brent Burket,
Robin D'Amato, Stephen Flanagan,
Joyce Gaskin, Cheryl Golding,
Maria Jimenez, Joe Justus,
Vincent McDonough, Yolanda
Miley, Maureen Morgan, Jovito
Pagkalinawan, Monica Reece,
Julie Riley, Martin Smith

We are grateful to our loyal *We Believe* users whose insights and suggestions have inspired **PROJECT DISCIPLE**—the premier faith formation tool built on the six tasks of catechesis.

Contents

SEASONAL CHAPTERS

UNIT 2

We Are Members of the Church

UNIT 3

The Church Leads Us in Worship

SEASONAL CHAPTERS

UNIT 4

We Are Called to Discipleship

22 We Continue the Work of Jesus

• Jesus brings God's life and love to all people.
• Jesus shares his mission with his disciples.
• The Church works for justice and peace.
• We live out the Good News of Jesus Christ.

John 20:19, 21; Luke 4:16–19

As Catholics .... Missionaries

PROJECT DISCIPLE *featuring* Supporting Missionary Work
Take Home Working for peace and justice
Chapter Test

23 The Church Respects All People

• People around the world have different beliefs about God. • The Jewish faith is important to Christians. • Christ calls his followers to be united.
• The Church works for Christian unity.

John 17:20–21

As Catholics .... Christian Unity

PROJECT DISCIPLE *featuring* Respect for all people
Take Home Respecting different faiths
Chapter Test

24 The Church Is Worldwide

• The Catholic Church is all over the world. • Catholics share the same faith. • Catholics celebrate their faith in different ways. • We are the light of the world.

Luke 4:42–43; Matthew 5:14, 16

As Catholics .... The Baptismal Register

PROJECT DISCIPLE *featuring* One Faith, Many Languages
Take Home Identifying family customs
Chapter Test

25 We Are God's Holy People

• We belong to the Communion of Saints. • Mary is the greatest of all the saints. • The Church remembers and honors Mary. • God calls us to be saints.

Luke 1:38

As Catholics .... Being canonized a saint

PROJECT DISCIPLE *featuring* Praying for the Dead
Take Home Praying to Mary
Chapter Test

26 The Kingdom of God Continues to Grow

• Jesus used parables to teach about the Kingdom of God. • Jesus taught that the Kingdom of God will grow. • Jesus' miracles were signs of the Kingdom of God. • The Kingdom of God grows.

Luke 11:1; 13:18–19;
Matthew 13:3–8, 18–23; 14:22–33

As Catholics .... Saint Elizabeth of Hungary

PROJECT DISCIPLE *featuring* The Kingdom of God
Take Home Reading about the Kingdom
Chapter Test

PROJECT DISCIPLE RESOURCES

27 Easter

• In the Easter season, we celebrate the Resurrection of Jesus.
John 20:19–29

We Believe

The *We Believe* program will help us to
learn celebrate share and **live our Catholic faith.**

Throughout the year we will hear about many saints and holy people.

Saint Andrew Nam-Thuong

Saint Augustine

Saint Charles Lwanga

Saint Clare of Assisi

Saint Dominic Savio

Saint Edward the Confessor

Saint Elizabeth of Hungary

Saint Felicity

Saint Francis of Assisi

Saint Joan of Arc

Saint John the Apostle

Blessed Pope John XXIII

Blessed Pope John Paul II

Saint Katharine Drexel

Saint Louise de Marillac

Saint Lucy

Saint Martin de Porres

Martyrs of El Salvador—
Sisters Ita Ford, Maura Clarke, and Dorothy Kazel; Jean Donovan

Saint Nicholas

Our Lady of Guadalupe

Saint Paul

Saint Perpetua

Saint Peter Claver

Pope Saint Pius X

Saint Raphael the Archangel

Saint Stephen

Together, let us grow as a community of faith.

Welcome!

WE GATHER

✝ **Leader:** Welcome, everyone, to Grade 3
We Believe. As we begin each chapter,
we gather in prayer. We pray to God together.

Let us sing the
We Believe song!

🎵 We Believe,
We Believe in God

We believe in God;
We believe, we believe in Jesus;
We believe in the Spirit who gives us life.
We believe, we believe in God.

We believe in the Holy Spirit,
Who renews the face of the earth.
We believe we are part of a living Church,
And forever we will live with God.

We believe in God;
We believe, we believe in Jesus;
We believe in the Spirit who gives us life.
We believe, we believe in God.

When we see **We Gather** we also come together as a class.

means it's time to

think about
talk about
write about
draw about
act out

at home
in our neighborhood
at school
in our parish
in our world

Talk about your life right now. What groups do you belong to?

What does belonging to these groups tell other people about you?

Each day we learn more about God.

WE BELIEVE

We learn about

- the Blessed Trinity: God the Father, God the Son, and God the Holy Spirit
- Jesus, the Son of God who became one of us
- the Church and its history and teachings
- the Mass and the sacraments
- our call to discipleship.

We find out about the different ways Catholics live their faith and celebrate God's love.

When we see **We Believe** we learn more about our Catholic faith.

Whenever we see ✝ we make the Sign of the Cross. We **pray** and begin our day's lesson.

Each of these signs points out something special that we are going to do.

📖 is an open **Bible**. When we see it or something like this (John 17:20–21), we hear the Word of God. We hear about God and his people. We hear about Jesus and the Holy Spirit.

🏃 means we have an **activity**. We might

talk   **write**   **act**
draw
sing
work together   **imagine**

There are all kinds of activities! We might see 🏃 in any part of our day's lesson. Be on the lookout!

🎵 means it is time to **sing** or listen to music! We sing songs we know, make up our own songs, and sing along with those in our *We Believe* music program.

KeyWords means it is time to review the **important words** we have learned in the day's lesson.

As Catholics...

Each week, we discover something special about our faith in the **As Catholics** box. Don't forget to read it!

13

WE RESPOND

We can respond by

- thinking about ways our faith affects the things we say and do

- sharing our thoughts and feelings

- praying to God.

Then in our homes, neighborhood, school, parish, and world, we can say and do the things that show love for God and others.

 In this space, draw yourself as a *We Believe* third grader.

When we see **We Respond** we think about and act on what we have learned about God and our Catholic faith.

We are so happy you are with us!

We sharpen our disciple skills with each chapter's Project Disciple pages!

Show What you Know

We "show what we know" about each chapter's content. A disciple is always learning more about his or her faith.

Reality Check

Here we can express our ideas and choices.

More to Explore

We learn more about ways disciples are living out their faith.

PROJECT

Grade 3 Chapter 9

Pray Learn Celebrate Share Choose Live

Show What you Know

Unscramble the letters in the left column. Then match the words to complete the sentences in the right column.

DERCE _____

CSUTJEI _____

HICLAOCT CSAOLI _____

OSLSPTAE ERDEC _____

HRCHCU _____

The _____ is the Body of Christ on earth.

We profess our faith each time we pray the _____

_____ is treating everyone fairly and with respect.

A _____ is a statement of beliefs.

_____ teaching tells us that we are made in God's image and have certain human rights.

Celebrate! ♪

Read the words to the song, "They'll Know We Are Christians" on page 107. Write your own song that tells of other ways that show we are Christians.

Now, pass it on!

webelieveweb.com

88

Reality Check

We are all part of the human family. That means we all have certain responsibilities to one another. What are your responsibilities?

- ❑ helping at home
- ❑ being a good friend
- ❑ sharing with your classmates
- ❑ participating at Mass
- ❑ other _____

More to Explore

Catholic Charities USA helps over ten million needy people throughout the United States each year. They offer groceries for those in need, counseling, daycare programs, and job training. They also work for justice for all people.

↳ **DISCIPLE CHALLENGE** Learn about Catholic Charities (www.catholiccharitiesusa.org), and share with your group.

Make it Happen

Think of someone who has taught you about your faith.

Tell what you learned _____

Now, pass it on!

Take Home

As a family act justly. Write ways your family can show respect for one another this week.

89

Celebrate!

As disciples, we worship God.

Make it Happen

We make sure that we "make faith happen" by living out what we have learned.

↳ **DISCIPLE CHALLENGE**

We take our disciple skills one step further.

Take Home

We always get the chance to share our faith "at home."

There are **LOADS** of **ACTIVITIES** that make us better disciples! Just look at this additional list.

What's the Word—all about Scripture

Question Corner—take a quiz

Fast Facts—learn even more about our faith

What Would You Do?—making the right choices

Pray Today—talking and listening to God

Picture This—ways for us to see and show our disciple skills

Saint Stories—finding great role models

Now, Pass It On!—invites us to witness to our faith

And every chapter ends with a Chapter Test!

PROJECT DISCIPLE

You are on a journey this year to become a disciple of Jesus Christ.

This year you will:

- **learn** what it means to belong to the Catholic Church.

- **pray** alone and with others.

- **celebrate** at Mass and in the sacraments, especially Eucharist and Penance.

- **choose** to respect all people as Jesus taught.

- **share** the Good News of the Kingdom of God.

- **live out** the faith by working for unity and growing in holiness.

Have a great year!

WE BELIEVE

GRADE 3 DISCIPLE CONTRACT

As a disciple of Jesus, this year I promise to

_____

_____

Name

_____

Date

_____

And remember, you can always visit **www.webelieveweb.com** for all kinds of activities, games, study guides, and resources.

16

Jesus Gives Us the Church

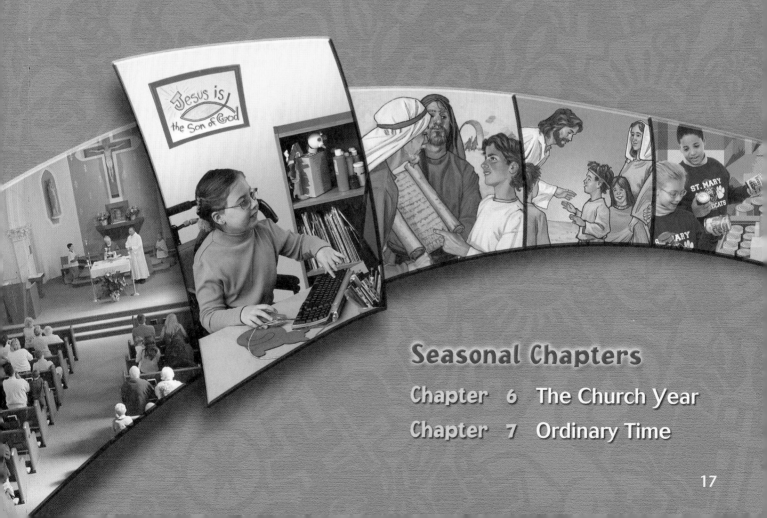

Seasonal Chapters

In Unit 1 your child will grow as a disciple of Jesus by:

- understanding that the Son of God became one of us and showed us how to live
- helping to spread the Kingdom of God as Jesus asked us to do
- recognizing that Jesus died, has risen, and will come again
- appreciating that the Holy Spirit came to the disciples on Pentecost and continues to help the Church
- following the example of the Apostles and our other ancestors in faith in leading lives of service and holiness.

Reality Check

"'The Christian family . . . can and should be called a *domestic church*.' It is a community of faith, hope, and charity."

(*Catechism of the Catholic Church*, 2204)

Celebrate!

Recall and share the story of your child's Baptism day. Now, as you did then, bless your child. Trace the sign of the cross on his/her forehead, saying this prayer:

*You were anointed with the chrism of salvation,
so that, united with his people,
you may remain for ever a member of Christ
and a faithful disciple.
Amen.*

Saint Stories

In Chapter 5, the children will learn about Saint Augustine. As a young man he was not very interested in God. His mother, Monica, prayed that he would turn to God. He finally did and was baptized. Reflect on your own constancy in prayer, and encourage your children to have patience and perseverance in prayer.

What's the Word?

Jesus calmed a storm at sea. Read the story from Mark 4:35–41. Talk about any fears your child might have, and explain that Jesus is with us always. When we are afraid, he can calm our fears.

Fast Facts

Jesus was baptized by John in the Jordan River. This river runs along the borders of Israel, the West Bank, and the kingdom of Jordan. The river is 156 miles long and flows through the Sea of Galilee where Jesus frequently visited. Today, the Jordan River is polluted. But groups like EcoPeace/ Friends of the Earth Middle East are working to clean and restore the Jordan River and possibly construct a Peace Park along its banks.

Take Home

Be ready for:

Chapter 1: Praying as a disciple

Chapter 2: Making a Bible bookmark

Chapter 3: Choosing ways to love

Chapter 4: Planning your prayer space

Chapter 5: Learning about saints

God Sends Us His Own Son

WE GATHER

Leader: Let us be very still and listen to this story of God's invitation to Mary to become the mother of Jesus:

Luke 1:26–35

In the sixth month, the angel Gabriel was sent to Mary. The angel told Mary that she would have a son and said to her, "You shall name him Jesus." (Luke 1:31) This child will be the Son of God.

All: Loving Father, thank you for the gift of your Son, Jesus. Thank you for choosing Mary to be his mother.

Leader: Let us pray.

Side 1: Jesus is the Son of God, alleluia.

Side 2: Jesus is the son of Mary, alleluia.

Side 1: He has come to save us all, alleluia.

Side 2: He has come to save us all, alleluia.

Who is someone special in your life? How do you show that this person is important to you?

WE BELIEVE
God the Son became one of us.

We believe in the Blessed Trinity. The **Blessed Trinity** is the Three Persons in One God: God the Father, God the Son, and God the Holy Spirit. God the Father wants us to know his love. So he sent his only Son to be with us. God the Son, the Second Person of the Blessed Trinity, became man. This truth is called the **Incarnation**.

God chose Mary to be the Mother of his Son and Joseph to be his Son's foster father. The Son of God was named Jesus. *Jesus* means "God saves."

Jesus is true God and true man. He is truly the Son of God. So Jesus is divine. *Divine* is a word we use to describe God. Jesus is truly the son of Mary. So Jesus is human. He is like us in all things except this: He is without sin.

How did God the Father show us his great love?

Jesus grew up in Nazareth.

Jesus grew up in the town of Nazareth in Galilee. He was a Jew. During Jesus' time, mothers like Mary would teach their children how to pray. They would tell them wonderful stories of their ancestors, the Jewish People who lived before them.

Key Words

Blessed Trinity (p. 250)

Incarnation (p. 251)

Sons learned what their fathers did for a living. Joseph was a carpenter. Jesus learned from Joseph how to work with wood and build things. So in the Bible Jesus is called "the carpenter's son." (Matthew 13:55)

 Luke 2:41–51

When Jesus was twelve years old, he went to Jerusalem to celebrate a Jewish feast with Mary, Joseph, and their relatives. After the celebration "the boy Jesus remained behind in Jerusalem, but his parents did not know it." (Luke 2:43)

Mary and Joseph searched everywhere for Jesus. They did not know that he was in the Temple talking with some teachers. Everyone was amazed at the questions Jesus asked. When Mary and Joseph found Jesus, they were surprised, too. They wanted him to return to Nazareth. Jesus obeyed and went with them.

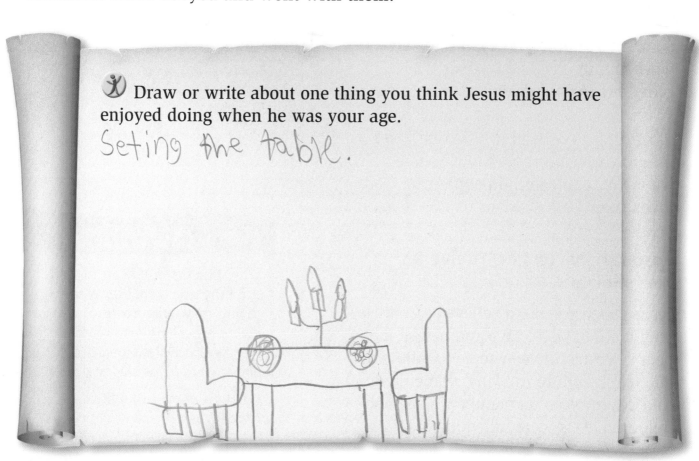

Draw or write about one thing you think Jesus might have enjoyed doing when he was your age.

Seting the table.

Jesus begins his work.

Jesus had a cousin named John. John was a prophet. A **prophet** is someone called by God to speak to the people.

John prepared the people for Jesus. He told them, "Repent, for the kingdom of heaven is at hand!"(Matthew 3:2). **Repent** means to turn away from sin and to ask God for help to live a good life.

John, called John the Baptist, baptized many people. This washing with water was a sign of their turning away from sin and their turning to God.

Even though Jesus was without sin, he went to John to be baptized. As Jesus came out of the water, God the Holy Spirit came upon him like a dove. A voice was heard saying, "This is my beloved Son, with whom I am well pleased." (Matthew 3:17)

Soon after this Jesus began his own work among the people. This was called his **public ministry**.

Prophets remind us that God loves us and cares for us. What are some ways you can remind people that God loves them?

Jesus shows us how to live as his followers.

Jesus called people to believe in God. He taught about God's love and healed many people. Jesus invited people to follow him and learn from him. Many women and men said yes to Jesus' invitation. Those who followed Jesus were called his **disciples**.

As Catholics...

When the first followers of Jesus used the title *Lord*, they were saying they believed Jesus was divine. By calling Jesus *Lord* people showed their respect for and trust in Jesus' divine power.

What are some other titles we have for Jesus?

In his ministry, Jesus tried to reach out to those who were ignored by others. He healed the sick and fed the hungry. He spent time with the poor and lonely. Jesus showed us how to be his disciples by the way he lived.

Jesus showed his love for God his Father by praying often. Once Jesus went by himself to a mountain to pray. He spent the whole night there in prayer. The next day, he called his disciples together and chose twelve men to be his Apostles. The word **Apostle** means "one who is sent."

Jesus' Apostles shared in his life and his work in a special way. They traveled with Jesus and became his close friends. They helped him teach and spread the message of God's love.

WE RESPOND

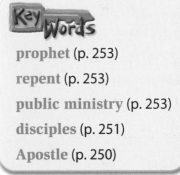 Use the computer screen below to design a Web page. Use words and drawings to show people from all over the world some ways to follow Jesus.

Key Words

prophet (p. 253)

repent (p. 253)

public ministry (p. 253)

disciples (p. 251)

Apostle (p. 250)

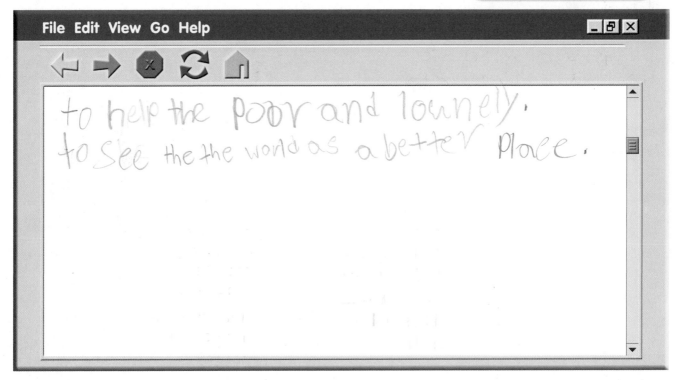

File Edit View Go Help

to help the poor and lounely.
to see the the world as a better place.

PROJECT

Show What you Know

Use the number code to find Key Words learned in this chapter.

A	B	C	D	E	H	I	L	M	N	O	P	R	S	T	U	Y
1	2	3	4	5	6	7	8	9	10	11	12	13	14	15	16	17

A P O S T L E
1 12 11 14 15 8 5

P U B L I C   M I N I S T R Y
12 16 2 8 7 3   9 7 10 7 14 15 13 17

I N C A R N A T I O N
7 10 3 1 13 10 1 15 7 11 10

P R O P H E T
12 13 11 12 6 5 15

B L E S S E D   T R I N I T Y
2 8 5 14 14 5 4   15 13 7 10 7 15 17

D I S C I P L E S
4 7 14 3 7 12 8 5 14

R E P E N T
13 5 12 5 10 15

↳ **DISCIPLE CHALLENGE** Circle the word that tells what the prophet John asked people to do.

More to Explore

The Holy Childhood Association invites children to help one another. One way to help is by collecting food, toys, clothing, or money for families in need. Visit their Web site at www.hcakids.org.

DISCIPLE

Pray
Learn
Celebrate
Share
Choose
Live

Picture This

What does the name Jesus mean? Color the spaces with a ● and you will find the answer!

Pray Today

Pray this prayer as a disciple of Jesus.

Jesus, you invite me to be your disciple.
You showed me how to love God the Father
with all my heart, with all my soul,
*   and with all my mind.*
You showed me how to love my neighbors
and the importance of loving myself.

It is not always easy to be a disciple.
I am grateful for the example you have
*   given to me.*
Jesus, continue to guide me
and strengthen me on my journey
*   to be your disciple. Amen.*

Now, pass it on!

Make it Happen

Write one way that your class can help families in need in your parish and neighborhood.

_____

Take Home

Jesus took time to pray every day. Look at the *Pray Today* prayer. Make a copy, and place it in your home. Pray it together this week.

CHAPTER TEST

Fill in the circle beside the correct answer.

1. The _____ is the Three Persons in One God.
   ○ Incarnation   ○ Bible   ● Blessed Trinity

2. The _____ is the truth that the Son of God became man.
   ○ Incarnation   ● Bible   ○ Blessed Trinity

3. The name Jesus means "_____."
   ○ God gives   ○ God loves   ● God saves

4. A _____ is someone called by God to speak to the people.
   ○ carpenter   ● prophet   ○ follower

Write T if the sentence is true. Write F if the sentence is false.

5. __T__ Jesus is both divine and human.

6. __F__ Jesus never prayed.

7. __F__ Jesus chose twelve men to be his Apostles.

8. __F__ When we repent, we turn to sin.

Write sentences to answer the questions.

9. What did John the Baptist do to prepare people for Jesus' coming?

   _____

10. What is one thing Jesus did in his public ministry?

   _____

Jesus Teaches Us About God's Love

2

WE GATHER

Leader: Let us gather together to pray.

🎵 **Lift High the Cross**

All: Lift high the cross,
the love of Christ proclaim
Till all the world adore his sacred name.

Leader: The same Lord is Lord
of all, giving to all who call upon him.
For "everyone who calls on the name of
the Lord will be saved." (Romans 10:13)

All: Lift high the cross,
the love of Christ proclaim
Till all the world adore his sacred name.

How can you show that you love
your family? How do your family
members show their love for you?

Jesus tells us how much God loves us.

Jesus taught that God loves each one of us. There are many examples of God's great love. We can read about them in the Bible. The Bible is a collection of books about God's love for us and about our call to live as God's people. It is also called *Scripture*.

The Bible has two parts, called *testaments*. The Old Testament is about the people of God before the time of Jesus. The New Testament is about the life of Jesus Christ and the beginning of the Church.

The human writers of the Bible were guided by God the Holy Spirit, the Third Person of the Blessed Trinity. Though the human writers chose the words, they wrote about things that God wanted to share with us. So the **Bible** is the book in which God's Word is written.

Talk about your favorite story about Jesus from the Bible.

Jesus teaches about the Kingdom of God.

Jesus must have been a wonderful teacher. We learn from the Bible that crowds followed him to hear what he had to say. Jesus often taught about the **Kingdom of God**, which is the power of God's love active in the world. Jesus wanted everyone to change their lives and turn to God.

Jesus taught about God's forgiveness and mercy. He taught about love and respect for others.

Jesus' greatest teaching was the way he lived. Jesus said that he "did not come to be served but to serve." (Mark 10:45) He wants us to do the same. He wants us to love one another as he loves us.

 Write or draw your own ending to this sentence:

The Kingdom of God is not like the kingdoms we read about in books or see in movies. The Kingdom of God is

Key Words

Bible (p. 250)
Kingdom of God (p. 251)

Jesus teaches about the gift of faith.

Faith is a gift from God that helps us to believe and trust in him. Jesus teaches us about faith in God by his stories and his actions.

 Luke 17:5–6

One day Jesus was teaching. His Apostles asked him to give them more faith. Jesus replied, "If you have faith the size of a mustard seed, you would say to [this] mulberry tree, 'Be uprooted and planted in the sea,' and it would obey you." (Luke 17:6)

A mustard seed is very tiny. It is about the size of the tip of a pencil. A mulberry tree is very strong. Imagine being able to make this tree lift itself into the sea!

Jesus was telling his Apostles that faith is very powerful. Faith allows us to believe what we cannot see or feel or touch.

🏃 Write one way other people share their faith with you.

_____

_____

As Catholics...

Mary is a great example of faith. Throughout her entire life she always believed in God. When the angel Gabriel appeared to her, Mary was told that God had chosen her to be the Mother of Jesus, God's own Son. Trusting in God, Mary said, "Behold, I am the handmaid of the Lord. May it be done to me according to your word." (Luke 1:38)

The Mulberry Tree by Vincent van Gogh

Jesus dies and rises to save us.

Jesus lived his life in such a way that people knew he loved God. Some powerful people hated Jesus because of what he did and said.

 Luke 23:33, 34

Jesus was arrested and put to death. Like a criminal, Jesus was **crucified**, nailed to a cross. Yet even as he was dying, Jesus prayed, "Father, forgive them, they know not what they do." (Luke 23:34)

Mary, the Mother of Jesus, and other women disciples stayed by Jesus' cross with John the Apostle. The other disciples hid because they were afraid. After Jesus died, his body was laid in a tomb.

 Luke 24: 1–12

Early Sunday morning some women returned to the tomb. They were carrying oils and spices to anoint the body of Jesus. When they reached the tomb, they saw that it was empty. The body of Jesus was not there!

Two men in dazzling garments told the women, "He is not here, but he has been raised." (Luke 24:6) The women went and told the Apostles the news.

We call Jesus' being raised from the dead the **Resurrection**. Jesus died and rose so that all people could be saved and live with God forever.

Key Words

faith (p. 251)

crucified (p. 250)

Resurrection (p. 253)

WE RESPOND

Pretend you were with the women who went to the tomb. How would you have felt? What would you have done and said? Act it out.

PROJECT

Show What *you* Know

Use the **Key Words** to complete the crossword puzzle.

Down

1. the book in which God's Word is written

2. how Jesus was put to death

Across

3. Jesus being raised from the dead

4. a gift from God that helps us to believe and trust in him

5. the power of God's love active in the world

Down 1. b i b l
Down 2. c r u c i f i e
Across 3. r e s u r r e c t i o n
Across 4. f a i t h
Across 5. K i n g d o m o f g o d

Fast Facts

Jesus often taught near the Sea of Galilee, which is Israel's largest fresh water lake.

Pray
Learn
Celebrate
Share
Choose
Live

Reality Check

Check the ways we can help spread the Kingdom of God.

- ☑ welcome a new neighbor
- ☑ help a friend to understand this lesson
- ☑ lie about something
- ☑ pray for others
- ☑ forgive someone
- ☑ be a bully

- ☐ _____

Now, pass it on!

More to Explore

An important part of our Catholic faith is the Bible, the Word of God. When we celebrate the sacraments, we listen to readings from the Bible. At these celebrations, we hear about God's never-ending love for his people. Each day the Word of God can come alive in our lives if we are listening to what God has to say to us.

↳ **DISCIPLE CHALLENGE** The next time you are at Mass, pay special attention to the readings.

Take Home

Make a Bible bookmark for your family. Use a piece of stiff paper and cut out a long strip. On one side, copy these words:

"Give thanks to the LORD,
   who is good,
   whose love endures forever."
   Psalm 118:1

Decorate both sides. Punch a small hole in the bottom center and tie a ribbon through the hole. Keep it in your Bible.

CHAPTER TEST

Write T if the sentence is true. Write F if the sentence is false.

1. __F__ The Old Testament of the Bible is about the life of Jesus Christ.

2. __T__ Jesus' greatest teaching was the way he lived.

3. __T__ Everyone who listened to Jesus liked him and believed in him.

4. __F__ Jesus died and rose so that all people could be saved.

Fill in the circle beside the correct answer.

5. _____ is God's gift that helps us to believe and trust in him.
   - ● Faith
   - ○ Fear
   - ○ Anger

6. The human writers of the Bible were guided by _____.
   - ○ Matthew
   - ● the Holy Spirit
   - ○ the disciples

7. The _____ is the power of God's love active in the world.
   - ○ Bible
   - ● Our Father
   - ○ Kingdom of God

8. Jesus' being raised from the dead is the _____.
   - ○ the tomb
   - ● Resurrection
   - ○ Kingdom of God

Answer the following.

9–10. Write two things Jesus told his disciples about faith.

_____

_____

Christ Will Come Again

3

WE GATHER

✝ **Leader:** Let us listen to the words of Jesus in Saint Matthew's Gospel:

Reader: "For I was hungry and you gave me food, I was thirsty and you gave me drink, a stranger and you welcomed me, naked and you clothed me, ill and you cared for me, in prison and you visited me." (Matthew 25: 35–36)

The Gospel of the Lord.

All: Praise to you, Lord Jesus Christ.

🎵 **Whatsoever You Do**

Chorus
  Whatsoever you do
    to the least of my people,
  that you do unto me.

  When I was hungry,
    you gave me to eat;
  When I was thirsty,
    you gave me to drink.
  Now enter into the home
    of my Father. (Chorus)

☀ Have you ever heard about someone who has special power? Describe what that person could do.

WE BELIEVE

Jesus has power over life and death.

Jesus loved his friends. Among his best friends were Martha, Mary, and their brother Lazarus. This family lived in a town called Bethany.

 John 11:1–3, 17–44

One day Lazarus became very sick. His sisters sent a message to Jesus telling him about Lazarus. When Jesus reached Bethany, Lazarus had already died and been buried.

Martha cried to Jesus that, if he had been there, he could have cured Lazarus. Jesus said, "I am the resurrection and the life; whoever believes in me, even if he dies, will live." Martha told Jesus, "I have come to believe that you are the Messiah, the Son of God." (John 11:25, 27)

Mary, Lazarus's other sister, came to greet Jesus. She was also crying. The sisters showed Jesus where Lazarus was buried, and Jesus began to cry.

A huge rock lay across the entrance to the place where Lazarus was buried. Jesus ordered that it be taken away. Then Jesus cried out in a loud voice, "Lazarus, come out!" (John 11:43) With that, Lazarus came out.

Jesus had raised Lazarus from the dead and more people began to believe that Jesus was the Messiah, the Son of God.

Jesus is the Resurrection and the life. If he asked you, "Do you believe this?" what would you say?

36

Jesus will come again.

One day the disciples wanted Jesus to tell them when the world would end. But Jesus said, "Stay awake! For you do not know on which day your Lord will come." (Matthew 24:42)

Jesus did not mean that our bodies should never go to sleep. He meant that we should always be preparing for his coming. We do this through prayer and the things we say and do.

Jesus' birth in Bethlehem is called his *first coming*. Jesus will come again at the end of time, and we will see him for ourselves. Jesus' coming at the end of time will be a joyful event. It is called his **second coming**.

When Christ comes again, we will be filled with joy and happiness. We will know Jesus because we will see him. Our life with the risen Christ will go on in joy forever.

As Catholics...

Jesus' raising Lazarus from the dead was a miracle. Jesus' miracles—walking on water, calming the seas, healing the sick—went beyond human power. Each miracle was a call to believe that Jesus was sent by God to save his people. Jesus' miracles were special signs that helped people to trust and believe in God. They showed people that God's Kingdom was present in their lives.

 We can "stay awake" for the second coming of Jesus Christ by living each day the way he taught us. Write one way you will "stay awake" in faith this week.

help aroundthe hoese move

Key Word

second coming (p. 253)

When Jesus Christ comes again, he will judge all people.

People can choose to be with God or to turn away from God. These choices will determine whether people can be with God in Heaven or not. **Heaven** is life with God forever.

 Matthew 25:31–43

Jesus told his followers that at the end of time he will come in glory with all the angels. He will separate all the people into two groups, one to his right and one to his left.

Then he will tell the people on his right that they are blessed by his Father. He will say, "For I was hungry and you gave me food, I was thirsty and you gave me drink, a stranger and you welcomed me, naked and you clothed me, ill and you cared for me, in prison and you visited me." Then the people on his right will ask when they saw him like this. And he will say, "Amen, I say to you, whatever you did for one of these least brothers of mine, you did for me." (Matthew 25:35–36, 40)

Jesus will then tell those on his left to go away from him forever because they did not care for him when he was hungry, thirsty, a stranger, ill, unclothed, or in prison.

When we choose to love and care for other people, especially those who are poor or weak, we love and care for Jesus. At the Last Judgment we will be judged by the way we treated others. The **Last Judgment** is Jesus Christ coming at the end of time to judge all people.

Key Words

Heaven (p. 251)

Last Judgment (p. 251)

👤 Name one way your parish can care for Jesus by caring for others.

care fore yofe hreabor as your self

Jesus teaches us to love others.

Jesus lived his life in perfect love of God the Father and in service to others. He is our example of holiness.

 Mark 12:28–32

One day, a man asked Jesus which commandment was the greatest. Jesus replied, "'You shall love the Lord your God with all your heart, with all your soul, with all your mind, and with all your strength.' The second is this: 'You shall love your neighbor as yourself.' There is no other commandment greater than these." (Mark 12:30–31)

If we love God with all of our heart and we love others as we love ourselves, we are choosing to follow Jesus. Jesus can help us make the right choices. He can give us the courage to treat others as we would like to be treated.

We all have chances to be good neighbors. Act out how you can be a good neighbor in the situation shown on this page.

WE RESPOND

In a group talk about why you think Jesus told us that love is the most important thing of all.

LOVE GOD! LOVE YOUR NEIGHBOR AS YOURSELF

PROJECT

Show What *you* Know

Write the **Key Word** that matches each definition.

> Heaven
>
> second coming
>
> Last Judgment

1. Jesus' coming at the end of time

second _coming_

2. Jesus Christ coming at the end of time to judge all people

last _judyment_

3. Life with God forever

Heaven

What Would *you* do?

Walk the path of a disciple today.
Write what you will do.

start

Get ready for
shool

Go to School

eat lunch

at class

resess

Pray
Learn
Celebrate
Share
Choose
Live

Make *it* Happen

Jesus told his disciples to "stay awake" so that they would be ready when he comes again. Wake up to the beauty of the world around you. Make a "wonder-full" list. Each day for a week, write about a gift of God's creation. Tell how you will take care of this gift, and how you can share this gift.

Celebrate!

Lead your family or class in this prayer.

Let us proclaim our faith.

Save us, Savior of the world,
(*All bow from the waist.*)

for by your Cross and Resurrection
(*All stand.*)

you have set us free.
(*All raise their hands in the air.*)

A Wonder-full Week

Sunday:_____

_____

Monday:_____

_____

Tuesday:_____

_____

Wednesday:_____

_____

Thursday:_____

_____

Friday:_____

_____

Saturday:_____

_____

Take Home

Take a family poll. Ask each member of your family to name one way to love God, themselves, and others.

CHAPTER TEST

Use the words in the box to complete the sentences.

1. Jesus' coming at the end of time is

   his _Second coming_.

2. Life forever with God is _Heaven_.

3. Jesus Christ coming at the end of time to judge all

   people is the _Last Judgment_.

Heaven
Last Judgment
second coming

Write T if the sentence is true. Write F if the sentence is false.

4. _F_ Jesus does not have power over sin and death.

5. _T_ We can make the choice to follow Jesus.

6. _T_ Jesus' coming at the end of time will be a joyful event.

Write sentences to answer the questions.

7. Who was Lazarus?

   he was a man

8. How will Jesus judge us at the end of time?

   he will judge by the way people treated others

9–10. What are two things Jesus taught us about loving God and others?

   that you should care for everson
   care for the pore

The Church Begins

4

WE GATHER

✝ **Mary:** Come, my children, let us pray.
There will come to us this day
The Helper who will show the way.

All: Let us wait and let us pray.

Peter: Listen, listen, do you hear
A wind that is blowing strong and clear?

Andrew: A wind that seems to stir in me
No longer fear, but bravery.

James: Look, look, above each the same,
A burning fire, a glowing flame.

John: And we are filled with great desire
To spread his word like a mighty fire.

All: Spirit of Jesus, fill us all
With life and love to heed your call.
Make us brave, strong, and true.
Disciples all, we will follow you.

Alleluia. Amen.

Think back to a time
when you were afraid of
something. Who or
what gave you the
courage to overcome
your fear?

WE BELIEVE

Jesus promises to send the Holy Spirit.

Jesus knew that his followers would be afraid when he had to leave them. So he promised to send them a special Helper, the Holy Spirit, who would always be with them.

 Matthew 28:16–20

Forty days after his Resurrection, Jesus met his Apostles in Galilee. It was their last meeting with him on earth. Jesus gave his Apostles a **mission**, or special job, to make disciples of all nations. The Apostles were to baptize people everywhere in the name of God the Father, the Son, and the Holy Spirit. Jesus said, "Behold, I am with you always, until the end of the age." (Matthew 28:20)

Then Jesus ascended and returned to his Father in Heaven. This event is called the **Ascension**. After Jesus' Ascension, his Apostles returned to Jerusalem. They did not know how they would ever be able to tell the whole world about Jesus.

Mary, the mother of Jesus, also returned to Jerusalem. She prayed with the Apostles and disciples as they waited for the coming of the Holy Spirit.

Think about the Apostles and disciples waiting for the Holy Spirit to come. How do you think they felt?

Pieter Coecke van Aelst (1502–1550), *Pentecost*

The Holy Spirit comes to the disciples.

Acts of the Apostles 2:1–41

Inside a room where they had gathered, the disciples heard a noise that sounded like a great wind. They saw what seemed to be flames of fire that spread out and touched each one of them. Suddenly, the disciples were filled with the Holy Spirit. They were changed in a wonderful way.

A large crowd was outside. The disciples came out of the room and began to speak about Jesus with great courage. Then Peter, the leader of all of the disciples, spoke to the people. He told them that God had raised Jesus from the dead. Peter told them that this Jesus who had been crucified and rose is truly the Lord, Jesus Christ.

When Peter spoke to the crowd, the people understood him in their different languages. They asked him what they should do. Peter replied, "Repent and be baptized, every one of you, in the name of Jesus Christ for the forgiveness of your sins; and you will receive the gift of the holy Spirit." (Acts of the Apostles 2:38) Many people accepted this message, and about three thousand people were baptized that day. The day on which the Holy Spirit came to the Apostles is called Pentecost. The Holy Spirit comes to us, too. The Holy Spirit helps us to be brave followers of Jesus.

In the flame, write words that describe how the disciples were changed when the Holy Spirit came to them.

Key Words

mission (p. 252)
Ascension (p. 250)
Pentecost (p. 252)

45

The Church begins on Pentecost.

On Pentecost, the disciples shared their Good News about Jesus with the people gathered around them. Soon, many people were baptized and received the Holy Spirit. This was the beginning of the Church. The **Church** is the community of people who are baptized and follow Jesus Christ.

The new believers listened to the teaching of the Apostles. They came together for prayer and for "the breaking of the bread" as Jesus and the Apostles did at the Last Supper. (Acts of the Apostles 2:42) They shared everything they owned with one another. They cared for those among them who were poor or in need. They treated everyone with love and respect.

Soon after the coming of the Holy Spirit, the Apostles and other disciples began to travel. They preached the Good News of Jesus to people in other cities and countries. Communities of new believers grew everywhere. Those people who were baptized began to be called **Christians**, because they were followers of Jesus Christ.

Key Words

Church (p. 250)

Christians (p. 250)

Imagine that you are back in the time of the first Christians. You have been asked to talk to a large crowd about following Jesus. Work with a partner on a speech that would tell them what to do.

46

The early Church grows.

As the Church grew, people in power began to worry that too many people were becoming Christians. At that time the disciple Stephen preached about Jesus. Because of Stephen, many people became Christians. The enemies of the Church were very angry, and they had Stephen put to death.

 Acts of the Apostles 9:3–5

Saul of Tarsus was one of the men determined to stop those who believed in Jesus. One day Saul was traveling along a road and a bright light from the sky suddenly flashed around him. He fell to the ground and heard a voice saying to him, "Saul, Saul, why are you persecuting me?" Saul wanted to know who was speaking to him. Then he heard, "I am Jesus, whom you are persecuting." (Acts of the Apostles 9:4, 5)

Saul's life changed forever. Three days later he was baptized. Saul, also known as Paul, became one of the greatest followers of Jesus Christ in history.

Paul made many trips to build up Christian communities throughout the world. His preaching and example encouraged many people to believe in Christ. His work and the work of many others helped the Church to grow. People of all races, languages, and nationalities came to believe in Jesus Christ.

As Catholics...

The Apostles and the first disciples told the Good News of Jesus Christ to everyone. This is called *evangelization*. We are called to go out and evangelize, too. Our pope and bishops want each of us to be a part of the "new evangelization." This means that the Good News of Jesus makes as much of a difference today as it did in the time of the first disciples.

WE RESPOND

We are too young to go all over the world telling people about Jesus Christ. But we can show the people in our neighborhood and parish family that we are followers of Jesus Christ. How can we do this?

_____

_____

_____

PROJECT

Pray
Learn
Celebrate
Share
Choose
Live

Show What *you* Know

Unscramble the words in column A.
Match these words with a clue in column B.

A

_____ 1. TSCIHARNSI _____

_____ 2. INSATNO _____

_____ 3. SNIMSOI _____

_____ 4. NSOAEISNC _____

_____ 5. UHCRHC _____

_____ 6. ISDEPISLC _____

_____ 7. ETPCNOETS _____

B

a. special job

b. Jesus' returning to the Father in Heaven

c. the day the Holy Spirit came upon the Apostles

d. community of people who are baptized and follow Jesus Christ

e. baptized people, followers of Jesus Christ

DISCIPLE CHALLENGE Use the unused words in column **A** to complete the following.

What was the Apostles' special job?

To make _____ of all _____.

Fast Facts

Today the Church proclaims the Good News of Jesus everywhere on earth and in every language. No matter where you are, the message of Jesus will always be the same.

SPREAD THE WORD

DISCIPLE

Pray
Learn
Celebrate
Share
Choose
Live

Picture This

Think about things that will help a disciple of Jesus stay healthy, keep the disciple informed, and lead the disciple on his or her journey of faith. Fill the backpack with these things.

Make it Happen

Share the Good News! Write a text message to tell a friend something you learned about your faith in this chapter.

Take Home

Think of a place in your home where your family can gather to pray. This will be your prayer space. What will it look like?

Write first, second, and third to tell the order in which the events happened.

1. Paul made many trips to Christian communities. _____

2. The Holy Spirit came upon the Apostles. _____

3. Jesus returned to his Father in Heaven. _____

Fill in the circle beside the correct answer.

4. The Holy Spirit came upon the disciples on _____.

   ○ the Ascension   ○ Easter   ○ Pentecost

5. All those who are baptized and follow Christ are called _____.

   ○ Apostles   ○ Christians   ○ brave followers

6. Jesus' returning to the Father in Heaven is _____.

   ○ the Ascension   ○ Easter   ○ Pentecost

Write sentences to answer the questions.

7. How does the Holy Spirit help us?

   _____

8. What was the mission Jesus gave to the Apostles?

   _____

9–10. What are two things the first members of the Church did as followers of Jesus?

   _____

   _____

We Learn About the Early Church

WE GATHER

✝ **Leader:** Let us gather in a prayer circle. Sit in a comfortable position.

Become still . . . still . . . still.

Close your eyes. Now, as you breathe out, whisper the name

Jesus

Jesus

Jesus.

Have you ever wanted to be a leader of a group or team? What does a leader do?

WE BELIEVE
The Apostles led the Church.

The Apostles lived with Jesus for three years. They knew how kind and caring he was. They ate and drank with him. They heard his words every day. They saw him heal the sick and raise the dead.

PHILIPPI

Wherever they went, the Apostles began to tell everyone about Jesus Christ. They baptized all those who believed in Jesus. In each place that they visited, the Apostles gathered these new Christians together. This is how they formed the Church. The Apostles had to move on to continue the work of Jesus so they chose leaders in each place.

There is a wonderful book in the New Testament that tells the story of the work of the Apostles in the early Church. It is called the **Acts of the Apostles**. In that book, we read that the early Christians listened to the teachings of the Apostles and looked after one another "according to each one's need." (Acts of the Apostles 2:45) The Church grew because Christians followed Jesus, loving and serving one another.

CORINTH

Name one way the Apostles were good leaders of the Church.

_____

_____

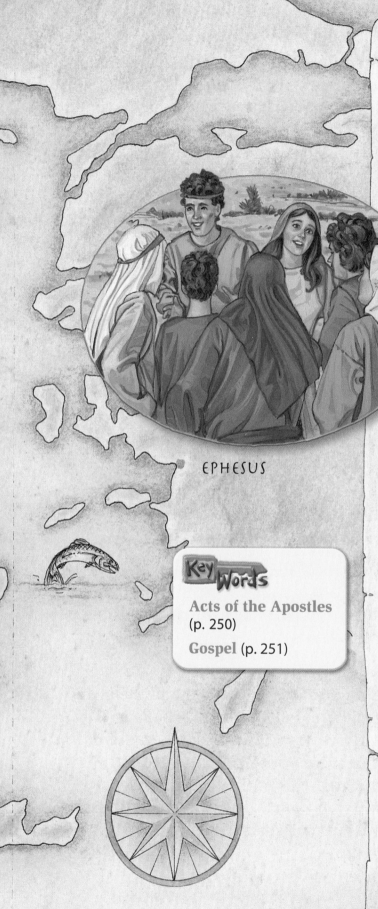

EPHESUS

Key Words

Acts of the Apostles
(p. 250)

Gospel (p. 251)

The disciples of Jesus share the Good News.

The followers of Jesus wanted everyone they met to know the Good News of Jesus Christ:

• Jesus is the Son of God. He came into the world to become one of us and show us, in person, the love of God.

• Jesus is the Savior of the whole world. All of us have been saved by the life, Death, and Resurrection of Jesus Christ.

Those who believed and accepted the Good News were baptized and became members of the Church. They listened to what the Apostles told them about Jesus and his teachings. They gathered together to share the Eucharist and "devoted themselves to the teaching of the apostles." (Acts of the Apostles 2:42)

Another word for "good news" is *gospel*. The Gospel is the Good News that we are saved by Jesus Christ, the Son of God. Like the first disciples, we are called to share the Gospel.

Work with a partner. On a strip of paper, write some Good News about Jesus that you wish to share with someone. Gather in a circle and share your Good News. Then make a Gospel chain.

As Catholics...

In Greek the word *fish, ichthus,* is made up of the first letters of "Jesus Christ," "Son of God," and "Savior." The fish was an important sign for the early Christians. They put this sign on the walls of places where they gathered to celebrate their faith. They also used it to mark the places where Christians were buried. Because it was a sign that the Romans did not use, Christians felt safe in using it. This simple sign stood for both the name and Good News of Jesus Christ.

The followers of Jesus stood up for their faith.

The Church began at a time when many countries were part of the Roman Empire. The Romans wanted everyone to worship their false gods. But the Christians would worship only the one, true God. Many Romans thought the Christians were a threat to the emperor's power. Soon the Christians were forced to worship Roman gods or face death.

The Roman leaders tried to make the Christians give up their faith in Jesus Christ. Many Christians were put in prison because they would not. Some Christians even died for their faith. We call people who die for their faith **martyrs**.

Name someone you know who stands up for his or her faith. Pray for that person.

Many of our ancestors in faith are examples of holiness.

Millions of Christians have lived before us. They are our ancestors in faith. Because of their holy lives the Church calls some of them saints.

Saints Perpetua and Felicity are two examples of holiness. Both of them were preparing to become Christians in the early years of the Church. Because of this they were arrested and treated terribly by the guards. Yet they both refused to worship Roman gods. They continued to believe in Jesus even when they were put to death.

Key Word

martyrs (p. 252)

Saint Augustine lived in North Africa. He was very popular when he was young. He was so busy enjoying himself that he never had time to think about God. As he grew older, he began to feel that his life had no meaning.

Augustine realized that God could give his life meaning. Augustine began to change. His love and need for God continued to grow. Augustine became a bishop and one of the Church's great writers.

These saints may have lived years ago, but their call to be holy is the same as ours is today.

Benozzo Gozzoli (1420–1497), *Saint Augustine*

WE RESPOND

How can you follow the saints who are our models of holiness? Circle the words in the letter box that will complete the sentences. Write the words on the lines provided.

```
F A I R J U S T
H E L P E X O H
A W O R S H I P
I T S A U M N D
R G O Y S R U O
```

We can tell others about _____.

We can _____ and _____ together, especially at Mass.

We can try to _____ others, especially those most in need.

We can be _____ and _____ to all people.

Pray Learn Celebrate Share Choose Live

PROJECT

Show What *you* Know

Starting with the first letter, cross out (X) every other letter to find the Key Word for each sentence.

> S A E C L T R S L O E F H T S H T E C A S P A O E S L T E L T E P S A

_____ is the book in the Bible that tells the story of the work of the Apostles in the early Church.

> L G E O P S G P O E S L G

_____ is the Good News that we are saved by Jesus Christ, the Son of God.

> S M R A Y R A T M Y A R T S y

_____ are people who die for their faith.

Question Corner

Imagine you were asked to interview one of the early Christians. Ask this person what it was like to be a disciple of Jesus during such difficult times. Then act out your interview.

DISCIPLE

Pray
Learn
Celebrate
Share
Choose
Live

Picture This

The fish was an important sign for the early Christians. It stood for both the name and the Good News of Jesus Christ. Decorate the poster to celebrate your faith in Jesus Christ.

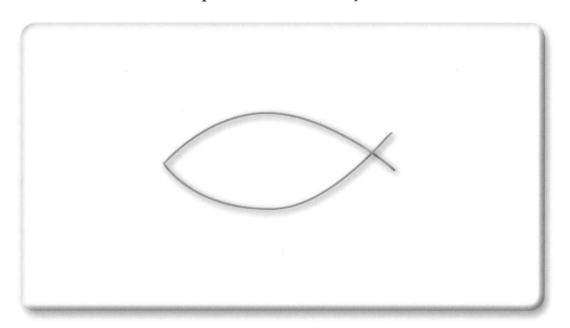

Celebrate!

The Church celebrates the Feast of All Saints on November 1. On this day, the Church remembers all the saints who are already celebrating God's life and love in Heaven. Write your own prayer of praise for all the holy men and women who have gone before us. Be sure to pray your prayer on All Saints' Day.

_____

_____

_____

_____

Take Home

With your family, visit *Lives of the Saints* on **www.webelieveweb.com**. Take time this month to learn about a saint each week. Pray to these saints at family meals.

CHAPTER TEST

Use the words in the box to complete the sentences.

1. _____ are people who die for their faith.

2. The _____ led the early Church.

3. _____ is a word that means "Good News."

4. _____, our ancestors in faith, are examples of holiness.

> Apostles
>
> martyrs
>
> saints
>
> Gospel

Write sentences to answer the questions.

5. Why does the Church honor Saints Perpetua and Felicity?

_____

6. Why does the Church honor Saint Augustine?

_____

7. What is the Acts of the Apostles?

_____

8. What is one thing the early Christians shared when they gathered together?

_____

9–10. What was the Good News that the disciples shared with everyone?

_____

_____

HOSANNA

"Hosanna!
Blessed is he who comes in
the name of the Lord!"

Mark 11:9

SEASONAL

CHAPTER 6

This chapter presents an overview of the
Church Year.

The Church year celebrates Jesus.

WE GATHER

What holidays do you and your family celebrate during the year? What holy days do you celebrate? Name some of your favorite days of celebration.

WE BELIEVE

All during the year, we gather to praise and thank God for his many gifts. We remember and celebrate the amazing things Jesus did for us. The seasons of the Church year help us to grow as followers of Jesus. The seasons help us to grow in faith.

Advent The season of Advent prepares us for the coming of the Son of God. We watch and wait. We prepare to celebrate the birth of Jesus Christ at Christmas.

Christmas The Christmas season is a time to celebrate that God is with us. We rejoice that the Son of God became one of us to save us.

Lent Lent is a season of preparation for the Church's greatest celebration. During the forty days of Lent, we pray for God's mercy and remember Jesus' life and Death.

The Three Days The Three Days celebrate the passing of Jesus from death to new life. The Three Days are the Church's greatest and most important celebration.

Easter Jesus has risen from the dead! During the Easter season, we celebrate the Resurrection of Jesus, for fifty days! Jesus is with us always.

Ordinary Time Ordinary Time is the season in which we celebrate the whole life of Jesus Christ and his teachings. It is the longest season of the year. It comes around twice—once between Christmas and Lent, and again after Easter until Advent.

Advent

Christmas

Ordinary Time

Ordinary Time

Lent

Three Days

Easter

 Look at the Church year time line on page 61. Then write the answers to these questions.

What is the shortest season of the year?	
What is the longest season of the year?	
In what season do we celebrate that Jesus rose from the dead and is with us always?	
What season of the year comes around twice?	
What season of the year are we in now?	
What season will we celebrate next?	

What is one great way to celebrate that Jesus is always with us?

✝ We Respond in Prayer

Leader: Blessed be the name of the Lord.

All: Now and for ever.

Reader: A reading from the holy Gospel according to Matthew

Jesus said to his disciples, "Behold, I am with you always, until the end of the age."
(Matthew 28:20)

The Gospel of the Lord.

All: Praise to you, Lord Jesus Christ.

Leader: Glory be to the Father, and to the Son, and to the Holy Spirit.

All: Now and for ever. Amen.

🎵 Jesus Is with Us

Chorus
Jesus is with us today,
Beside us to guide us today.
Jesus teaches us,
Jesus heals us, for we are his Church;
we are his chosen; we are the children of God.

Jesus teaches us to love one another,
To care for our brothers and sisters in need.
For when we show kindness to others,
We are God's children indeed. (Chorus)

PROJECT DISCIPLE

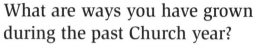

Celebrate! Which is your favorite Church season?
Now, pass it on!

Reality Check

What are ways you have grown during the past Church year?

❏ I have grown taller.

❏ I received my First Holy Communion.

❏ I have a new baby brother or sister.

❏ I learned a new prayer.

❏ I made a new friend.

❏ I received God's forgiveness in the Sacrament of Penance for the first time.

❏ I joined a sports team.

❏ I learned something about my faith.

❏ I have a new favorite TV show.

❏ I have a new pet.

❏ I read a good book.

Take Home

This year, in what season of the Church year do these family events fall?

Family Event	Season of the Church Year
My birthday _____	_____
First day of school _____	_____
My family's favorite holiday _____	_____

"Lord, it is good
to give thanks to you."

Responsorial Psalm, Eighth Sunday
in Ordinary Time

SEASONAL

CHAPTER 7

This chapter helps us to understand
the season of Ordinary Time.

In Ordinary Time, we celebrate the life and teachings of Jesus Christ.

WE GATHER

Can you remember the names of all the seasons in the Church year?

Which season is the Church in right now?

WE BELIEVE

Ordinary Time is a special time in the Church. During this season, we celebrate everything about Jesus! We hear about his teaching, his love, and his forgiveness. We also learn to be his followers.

Ordinary Time is the longest season of the Church year. It lasts about thirty-three or thirty-four weeks. It is called Ordinary Time because the weeks are "ordered," or named in number order. For example, the First Sunday in Ordinary Time is followed by the Second Sunday in Ordinary Time, and so on.

On the Sundays of Ordinary Time, and on the weekdays, too, the priest wears green vestments. Green is a sign of new life and hope.

On Sundays and weekdays in Ordinary Time, we learn about Jesus and his teachings by listening to the Scripture readings. Sometimes we hear events in the life of Jesus. Sometimes we hear a story Jesus told.

Together make a list of some of the events in the life of Jesus and a list of some stories he told.

_____

_____

_____

_____

Then in groups talk about your favorite events or stories. Act out one for the rest of the class.

During Ordinary Time, we learn more about Jesus and his teachings so that we can become more like him. Through the sacraments we share in his life. And we follow his example by praying, loving others, and working for justice and peace.

WE RESPOND

The events in the lives of the saints show us how to become more like Jesus, too. During Ordinary Time, the Church celebrates many feasts and remembers the holy lives of the saints.

Here are two feasts the Church celebrates in September.

The Feast of Saint Peter Claver
(September 9)

Saint Peter Claver was born in Spain. He became a priest of the Society of Jesus. He was sent to South America. There he helped the slaves who were arriving on ships from Africa each day. The slaves were treated badly on the ships. They were afraid and were often sick. Saint Peter helped them. He took care of their wounds and told them about Jesus. The slaves knew he was a true friend.

The Feast of the Exaltation of the Holy Cross
(September 14)

On this feast, we celebrate the cross of Jesus Christ as a sign of victory. We are signed with the cross in Baptism. We begin and end our prayers with the Sign of the Cross. The cross is a sign of Jesus' love for us.

✝ We Respond in Prayer

Leader: Let us pray now to honor the holy cross of Jesus. As we sing a song of joy and victory, let us process to our place of prayer.

🎵 **We Sing Your Glory**

We sing your glory,
    sing your praise.
We sing your glory,
    sing your praise.
We sing your glory,
    we sing your glory.
Glory, glory and praise!

Reader: "The grace of the Lord Jesus Christ and the love of God and the fellowship of the holy Spirit be with all of you."
(2 Corinthians 13:13)

All: And with your spirit.

Reader: Jesus, your cross is a sign of your love for us and for the whole world.

All: Jesus, make us signs of your love.

Leader: Father, we rejoice in the gifts of love we have received through the holy cross of Jesus your Son. Open our hearts to share his life and continue to bless us with his love. We ask this in the name of Jesus the Lord.

All: Amen.

Picture This

During Ordinary Time the Church celebrates the life and teachings of Jesus. Draw a story about Jesus from the Bible.

Pray Today

Jesus asks us to be a sign of hope to others. Pray this prayer each day this week.

Jesus,
You taught about God's kingdom
of love and peace.
Help me to watch for hopeful
signs of that kingdom today.
Remind me to show my love for
others even when I am tired
or busy.
Let me be a sign of your hope to
each person I meet.
I pray this in your holy name.
Amen.

Now, pass it on!

Take Home

During the season of Ordinary Time, we celebrate everything about Jesus, especially his love and forgiveness. Make a bumper sticker that encourages families to love and forgive.

Use the bumper sticker to start a conversation with your family. Talk about the ways families can be more loving and forgiving.

UNIT TEST

Fill in the circle beside the correct answer.

1. Jesus is both divine and _____.

   ○ unkind   ○ human   ○ sinful

2. The _____ is the Good News that we are saved by Jesus Christ.

   ○ Gospel   ○ Ascension   ○ Incarnation

3. Jesus prayed _____.

   ○ only in the night   ○ often   ○ once a day

4. When Jesus comes again, he will judge _____.

   ○ only sinners   ○ all people   ○ only his followers

5. _____ is life forever with God.

   ○ Heaven   ○ Faith   ○ Power

Use the terms in the box to complete the sentences.

6. Saints are our _____ in faith.

7. The _____ is the power of God's love active in the world.

8. The truth that God the Son became man is the

   _____.

9. Jesus' being raised from the dead is the

   _____.

10. The _____ is the Three Persons in One God.

| Kingdom of God |
| Resurrection |
| Blessed Trinity |
| ancestors |
| Incarnation |

continued on next page

Write sentences to answer the questions.

11. What was the mission Jesus gave the Apostles?

_____

12. What happened on Pentecost?

_____

13. What did Saint Paul do to help the Church?

_____

14. What are some of the things Jesus did in his public ministry?

_____

15. How can we follow Jesus' example?

_____

We Are Members of the Church

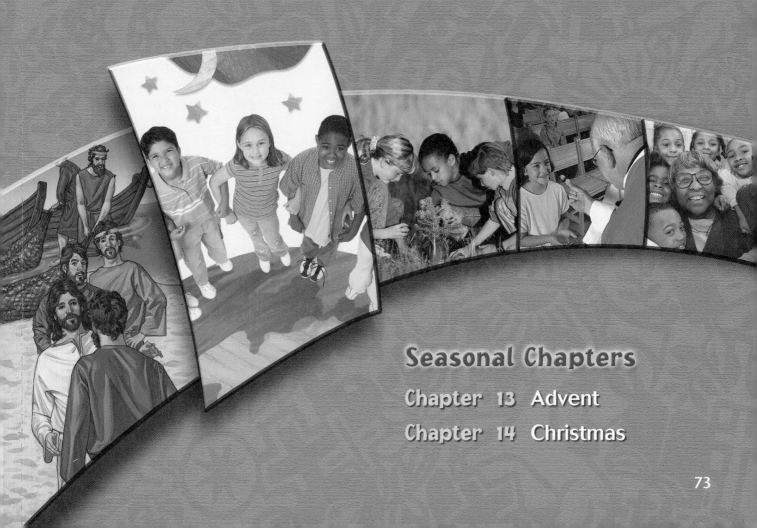

Seasonal Chapters

PROJECT DISCIPLE

DEAR FAMILY

In Unit 2 your child will grow as a disciple of Jesus by:

- learning that the pope and bishops lead the one, holy, catholic, apostolic Church
- recognizing that the Church is guided by the Holy Spirit to teach the truth
- praying alone and with others to praise God, thank God, ask for forgiveness, offer blessings, and seek God's help
- joining with our parish to worship God and to serve others
- appreciating the ways that people can grow in holiness as laypeople, ordained men, and religious.

Fast Facts

The Temple in Jerusalem was destroyed and rebuilt, and now archaeologists are working to discover what it was originally like. Part of one reconstruction remains—the Western Wall. People still go there to pray. They often write their prayers out and place them in the Wall.

Blessed Pope John Paul II at the Western Wall.

Question Corner

In Chapter 8 the children will learn about the four marks of the Church—*one, holy, catholic,* and *apostolic.* Complete the following:

Our parish is united when _____.

Our parish shows holiness when _____.

Our parish is welcoming when _____.

Our parish follows the teachings of Jesus and the Apostles by

_____.

Reality Check

"Authority, stability, and a life of relationships within the family constitute the foundations for freedom, security, and fraternity within society."

(*Catechism of the Catholic Church,* 2207)

More to Explore

Catholic Charities USA (see page 89) was founded in 1910. Through their work, they carry on the mission of Jesus. Visit their Web site to see some of their current work. Talk about the needs in your own community. What can your family do to respond?

Show That You Care

Chapter 12 talks about the ways we live as disciples of Jesus through different vocations. Find out if anyone in your parish is preparing to become a priest, deacon, religious brother or sister, or if there is a couple preparing for marriage. Put their names where you will remember to pray for them. You might even send a card to let them know you are praying for them!

Take Home

Be ready for:

Chapter 8: Listing family characteristics

Chapter 9: Talking about ways to show respect

Chapter 10: Choosing someone to pray for at Mass

Chapter 11: Praying for people who are sick

Chapter 12: Taking a holiness survey

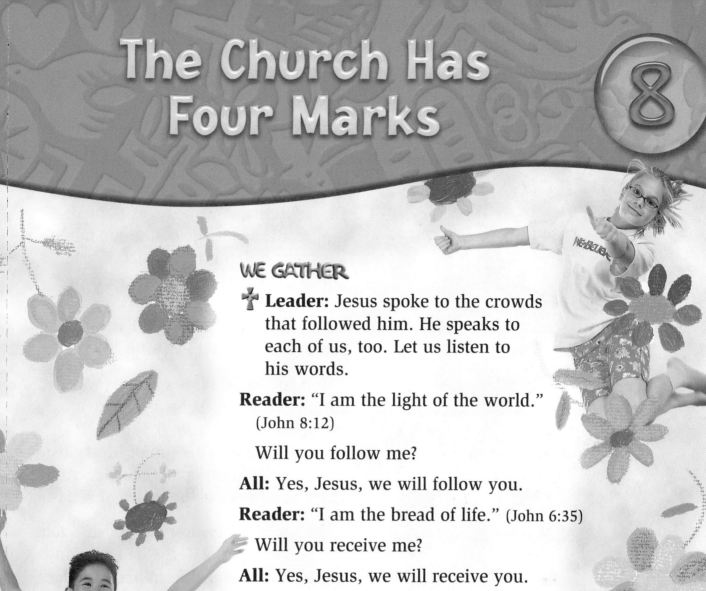

WE GATHER

✝ **Leader:** Jesus spoke to the crowds that followed him. He speaks to each of us, too. Let us listen to his words.

Reader: "I am the light of the world." (John 8:12)

Will you follow me?

All: Yes, Jesus, we will follow you.

Reader: "I am the bread of life." (John 6:35)

Will you receive me?

All: Yes, Jesus, we will receive you.

Reader: "I am the resurrection and the life." (John 11:25)

Do you believe in me?

All: Yes, Jesus, we believe in you. Amen.

☀ Think about the school teams or clubs that you can join. Who are the leaders of these groups? What do they do?

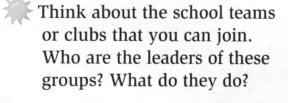

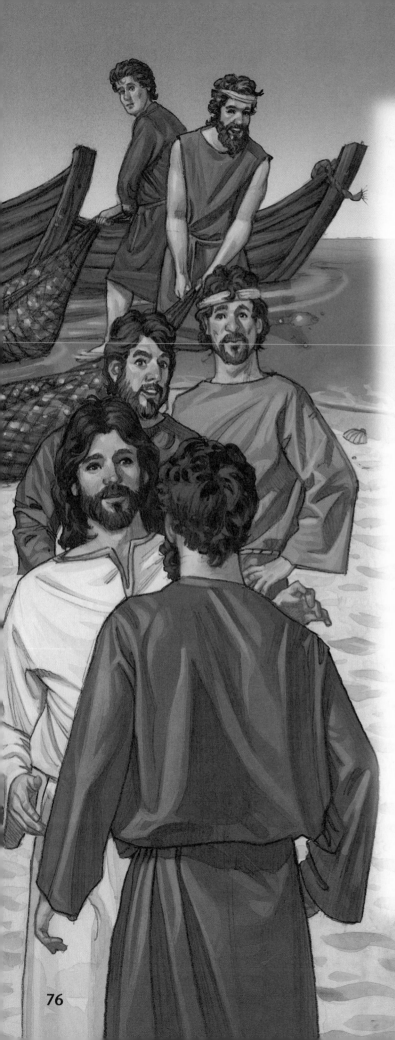

WE BELIEVE
Jesus chose the Apostles to lead the Church.

One of Jesus' Apostles was named Simon. Jesus changed Simon's name to Peter, which means "rock." Jesus chose Peter to be the leader of the Apostles. He told Peter, "You are Peter, and upon this rock I will build my church." (Matthew 16:18)

The Apostles are Peter, Andrew, James and John (sons of Zebedee), Philip, Bartholomew, Thomas, Matthew, James (the son of Alphaeus), Thaddeus, Simon, and Judas Iscariot. Later Matthias took the place of Judas.

After Jesus' Ascension the Apostles told the people all that Jesus had said and done. They traveled from place to place teaching what Jesus had taught them.

In every location the Apostles gathered the baptized into communities. The Church grew, and the first members of the Church looked to Peter and the Apostles as their leaders.

Look at the picture on page 77. In the space, write something you think the Apostle told people about Jesus.

What will you tell people you know about Jesus?

The pope and bishops are the successors of the Apostles.

Like Jesus, the Apostles chose leaders to succeed them. A *successor* is one who succeeds, or takes the place of, another. These new leaders would take the place of the Apostles and continue their work.

The Apostles gave these leaders the same authority that Jesus had given to them. Strengthened by the Holy Spirit, these leaders became the successors of the Apostles.

As time passed each of these leaders was given the title of bishop. **Bishops** are the successors of the Apostles. The bishops continue to lead the Church. They lead local areas of the Church called **dioceses**.

The **pope** is the bishop of the diocese of Rome in Italy. He continues the leadership of Peter. Together with all the bishops, he leads and guides the whole Catholic Church.

 Talk about what you know about your bishop, your diocese, and the pope.

Find out more about the pope and Vatican City. Check the Vatican Web site at www.vatican.net.

Key Words

bishops (p. 250)
dioceses (p. 251)
pope (p. 253)

As Catholics...

The pope lives in Vatican City, in Rome, Italy. He is the leader of the whole Catholic Church. So in a way the whole world is his parish. He goes to places around the world to teach the Good News of Jesus Christ and to seek peace. He encourages people to treat one another with respect. He also asks for help for those who are in need.

The Church is one and holy.

The Church is one, holy, catholic, and apostolic. We call these characteristics the **marks of the Church**.

The Church is *one*, a community called together by God. Through the Church, God strengthens us to live and worship together.

All members of the Church are united by Baptism. We gather to celebrate the sacraments. We share with one another and serve together.

The Church is *holy*. God is all good and holy. God shares his holiness with the Church. Through Baptism all members of the Church receive a share in God's life. This share in God's life makes us holy.

As members of the Church we grow in holiness when we celebrate the sacraments. We also grow in holiness when we love God and others as Jesus did.

What is one way the Church is a community?

Key Word

marks of the Church (p. 252)

78

The Church is catholic and apostolic.

The Church is *catholic*. The word *catholic* means "universal." The Church is open to all people. It is universal.

Jesus sent his Apostles out to every part of the world. They spread the Gospel to everyone, and the Church continued to grow. Even today people everywhere are invited and welcomed to become members of the Church. There are Catholics on every continent and in every country.

The Church is *apostolic*. The word *apostolic* comes from the word *apostle*. Jesus chose the Apostles to be the first leaders of the Church. Their mission was to teach the Good News and to baptize believers. By Baptism all members of the Church share in the work of spreading the Good News of Christ.

The bishops continue the mission of the Apostles in three very important ways.

- They *teach*. The bishops are the official teachers of the Church. They make sure that the members of the Church know and believe the teachings of Jesus.

- They *lead*. The bishops are the main leaders of the Church.

- They *sanctify*. The bishops work to make the People of God holy. They do this through prayer, preaching, and the celebration of the sacraments.

WE RESPOND

Draw a picture to show one of the four marks of the Church.

PROJECT

Show What you Know

Read the clues. Write the answers in the crossword puzzle.

Across

3. the Bishop of Rome, who leads the whole Catholic Church

5. local areas of the Church led by bishops

6. first mark of the Church

8. an Apostle whose name means "rock"

9. third mark of the Church

Down

1. four characteristics that describe the Church

2. fourth mark of the Church

4. the successors of the Apostles who lead the Church

7. second mark of the Church

DISCIPLE

Pray
Learn
Celebrate
Share
Choose
Live

Picture This

The Church is universal. This means it is open to all people. Design a pennant that shows that the Church welcomes people from all over the world.

Now, pass it on!

Make it Happen

At 76 years of age, Pope John XXIII gathered the bishops from all over the world for the Second Vatican Council (1962). Together they worked to strengthen the one, holy, catholic, and apostolic Church.

↳ **DISCIPLE CHALLENGE** Decide on a way to live out one mark of the Church.

_____

_____

Take Home

The Church has four marks or special characteristics. What makes your family special? Write your family characteristics.

The _____ Family

_____ _____

_____ _____

Fill in the circle beside each correct answer.

1. Jesus chose _____ to be the leader of the Apostles.

   ○ Matthias   ○ Peter   ○ Judas

2. Local areas of the Church are called _____.

   ○ bishops   ○ successors   ○ dioceses

3. The word _____ means "universal."

   ○ *catholic*   ○ *apostolic*   ○ *sanctify*

4. The pope and bishops are the _____ of the Apostles.

   ○ relatives   ○ dioceses   ○ successors

Complete the sentences by writing the correct mark of the Church: one, holy, catholic, and apostolic.

5. The Church is _____. All members of the Church are united by Baptism.

6. The Church is _____. It is open to all people.

7. The Church is _____. Through Baptism we receive a share in God's life.

8. The Church is _____. All members of the Church share in the mission Jesus gave the Apostles.

Answer the following.

9–10. Write two ways the pope and bishops carry on the work of the Apostles.

_____

_____

The Church Teaches Us

WE GATHER

✝ **Leader:** God, we are your people.

All: We are your Church.

Leader: Keep us faithful to you.

All: We are your faithful followers.

Leader: Help us to do your work on earth.

All: We want to share your Good News with others.

🎵 **They'll Know We Are Christians**

We will walk with each other,
We will walk hand in hand,
We will walk with each other,
We will walk hand in hand,
And together we'll spread the news
that God is in our land.
And they'll know we are Christians
by our love, by our love,
Yes, they'll know we are Christians
by our love.

☀ Name some good things about being a member of your family or your class.

83

WE BELIEVE

The Church is the Body of Christ and the People of God.

 1 Corinthians 12:14–21

Saint Paul explained to the people that the Church is the *Body of Christ* on earth. All the parts in a person's body work together. The ear does not say, "Because I am not an eye I do not belong to the body." The eye does not say to the hand, "I do not need you." (1 Corinthians 12:16, 21) Each part of the body needs all the other parts.

Like a human body, the Church has many parts, or members. One part cannot say to another, "I do not need you!" or "You are not like me, so you do not belong." Everyone in the Church is an important part of the Body of Christ. We are united through our love for and belief in Jesus Christ.

God has chosen us to be his children, brothers and sisters of Jesus. Through our Baptism, we are brought into the Church. In the New Testament the Church is described as "God's people." (1 Peter 2:10) As the *People of God*, we try our best to love God and love one another. We try to share the Good News of Jesus with everyone in the world.

Look at the pictures. How are these people showing that they are the People of God?

_____

_____

_____

_____

We profess our faith through the Apostles' Creed.

Apostles' Creed

I believe in God, the Father almighty,
    Creator of heaven and earth,

and in Jesus Christ, his only Son,
    our Lord,
who was conceived by the Holy Spirit,
born of the Virgin Mary,
suffered under Pontius Pilate,
was crucified, died, and was buried;
he descended into hell;
on the third day he rose again
from the dead;

he ascended into heaven,
and is seated at the right hand
    of God the Father almighty;
from there he will come to judge
    the living and the dead.

I believe in the Holy Spirit,
    the holy catholic Church,
    the communion of saints,
    the forgiveness of sins,
    the resurrection of the body,
    and life everlasting. Amen.

We state our belief in the Blessed Trinity: God the Father, God the Son, and God the Holy Spirit.

We state our belief that God the Son, the Second Person of the Blessed Trinity, became one of us and died to save us.

We state our belief in the holy Catholic Church that Jesus gave us. When we pray the Apostles' Creed we say together as the Church that we are one in faith and love.

As the Church grew, the beliefs about Jesus and his teachings were written down in statements called *creeds*. One of the first creeds is called the **Apostles' Creed**. It is based on the teachings of Jesus Christ and the faith of the Apostles.

Each time we pray the Apostles' Creed, we profess our faith. To *profess* means "to state what we believe."

Apostles' Creed
(p. 250)

With a partner talk about the ways we show our Catholic beliefs.

The Holy Spirit guides the Church.

Jesus knew it would be difficult for the Apostles to remember everything he had taught them. So he promised the Apostles that "the holy Spirit that the Father will send in my name—he will teach you everything and remind you of all that [I] told you." (John 14:26) With the help of the Holy Spirit, the Apostles were able to speak the truth about Jesus.

Today the Holy Spirit continues to guide the Church. The Holy Spirit guides the pope and bishops to teach the truth about Jesus. They do this by their words, writings, and actions. The pope and the bishops are the official teachers for the whole Church.

At certain times the pope gathers together all the bishops throughout the world. They make important decisions about the Church's faith and life.

Often the pope writes letters to the Church and to the whole world. These letters are about Catholic beliefs and how to live as Catholics in the world today.

Name something you have learned about Jesus and the Church. Who taught you?

The Church continues to teach the true message of Jesus.

The Church teaches what Jesus taught:

- God loves and cares for everyone.
- We are to love God with our whole heart.
- We are to love our neighbors as ourselves.

Some of the Church's teaching is known as *Catholic social teaching*. This teaching tells us that we are all made in God's image and have certain human rights. For example, we all have the right to life, food, housing, and safety. We have the right to be educated and to be treated equally.

These human rights are an important part of justice. **Justice** is treating everyone fairly and with respect. The justice that Jesus taught reminds us that we are all part of the human family. What helps or hurts one part of the family affects everyone.

We all have certain responsibilities to one another. For example, we have a responsibility to live together in peace. We have a responsibility to share the good things of the world. We have a responsibility to respect and care for one another.

WE RESPOND

What can you do this week to treat everyone fairly at home?

_____

in school?

_____

in your parish?

_____

Key Word

justice (p. 251)

As Catholics...

Francis of Assisi was the son of a rich merchant. In his twenties, Francis felt God calling him to a different way of life. Francis gave up his wealth and began to live a simple, poor life. He fasted, prayed, and helped the poor. He preached to people about following God. Other men joined Francis and shared his life of fasting, poverty, and peace. In 1210 Francis began a religious community now known as the Franciscans.

Also born in Assisi, Clare heard Francis preach. She wanted to live a simple, poor life for Christ like Francis did. She devoted her life to God. With the help of Francis, Clare began a religious order of nuns that is known as the Poor Clares. Both communities continue to serve the needs of God's people.

Saint Francis' feast day is October 4, and Saint Clare's is August 11.

PROJECT

Pray
Learn
Celebrate
Share
Choose
Live

Show What *you* Know

Unscramble the letters in the left column. Then match the words to complete the sentences in the right column.

DERCE _____ ●

● The _____ is the Body of Christ on earth.

CSUTJEI _____ ●

● We profess our faith each time we pray the

_____.

HICLAOCT CSAOLI

_____ _____ ●

● _____ is treating everyone fairly and with respect.

OSLSPTAE ERDEC

_____ _____ ●

● A _____ is a statement of beliefs.

HRCHCU _____ ●

● _____ teaching tells us that we are made in God's image and have certain human rights.

Celebrate!

Read the words to the song, "They'll Know We Are Christians" on page 83. Write your own song that tells of other ways that show we are Christians.

Now, pass it on!

_____

_____

_____

_____

_____

DISCIPLE

Pray
Learn
Celebrate
Share
Choose
Live

Reality Check

We are all part of the human family. That means we all have certain responsibilities to one another. What are your responsibilities?

- ❏ helping at home
- ❏ being a good friend
- ❏ sharing with your classmates
- ❏ participating at Mass
- ❏ other _____

More to Explore

Catholic Charities USA helps over ten million needy people throughout the United States each year. They offer groceries for those in need, counseling, daycare programs, and job training. They also work for justice for all people.

↳ **DISCIPLE CHALLENGE** Learn about Catholic Charities (**www.catholiccharitiesusa.org**), and share with your group.

Make it Happen

Think of someone who has taught you about your faith.

Tell what you learned _____

_____

_____.

Now, pass it on!

Take Home

As a family act justly. Write ways your family can show respect for one another this week.

_____

_____

_____

CHAPTER TEST

Write T if the sentence is true. Write F if the sentence is false.

1. _____ The Church is the Body of Christ.

2. _____ Justice is a statement of beliefs.

3. _____ The Holy Spirit helps the pope and bishops teach the truth about Jesus and our Catholic faith.

4. _____ We have a responsibility to care only about the Catholics in our diocese.

Write sentences to answer the questions.

5–6. What are two ways the pope and bishops teach the truth about Jesus?

_____

_____

7–8. What are two truths we say we believe when we say the Apostles' Creed?

_____

_____

9–10. What are two things Catholic social teaching tells us?

_____

_____

The Church Prays

10

WE GATHER

✝ **Leader:** Be still and quiet. Place your hands on your knees with your palms up.

Talk to God in your heart. Tell him anything you wish. Ask God for what you need, and ask his blessing on those you love.

All: (Pray quietly.)

Leader: Lift up your hands as a sign of your prayer rising to God.

All: Let my prayer be incense before you.

(Psalm 141:2a)

When someone you love is far away, how can you stay in touch?

WE BELIEVE
Jesus teaches his followers how to pray.

Jesus is the Son of God. Jesus is divine because he is God. He is also Mary's son. Jesus is human like us in every way except he is without sin.

Jesus had to learn how to walk, talk, read, and write. Mary and Joseph also taught Jesus how to talk to God in prayer. **Prayer** is listening and talking to God.

Jesus prayed in the **synagogue**, the gathering place where Jewish People pray and learn about God. Jesus also worshiped in the Temple in Jerusalem. Other times he went off by himself to pray. Sometimes he prayed with his family or his disciples.

The disciples wanted to learn how to pray as Jesus did. One day they said to him, "Lord, teach us to pray." (Luke 11:1) So Jesus taught them this prayer:

> Our Father, who art in heaven,
> hallowed be thy name;
> thy kingdom come;
> thy will be done on earth
>   as it is in heaven.
> Give us this day our daily bread;
> and forgive us our trespasses
> as we forgive those who trespass
>   against us;
> and lead us not into temptation,
> but deliver us from evil. Amen.

This prayer is the Lord's Prayer. We also call it the Our Father. It is the greatest example of prayer for the Church.

Use your own words to tell what we pray for when we pray the Lord's Prayer.

We can pray with others or by ourselves.

We often come together to worship God. We gather with others to celebrate the **liturgy**, the official public prayer of the Church. Each celebration of the liturgy is an action of the whole Church. Together as the Church, we worship the Blessed Trinity. We pray with Christ and with the whole Church, the Body of Christ.

Sometimes we pray alone just as Jesus did. We call this personal prayer. We can pray at any time and in any place. We can pray prayers such as the Our Father and the Hail Mary. We can also pray with our own words. God listens to us when we pray. He knows what we need.

Draw one way your family likes to pray.

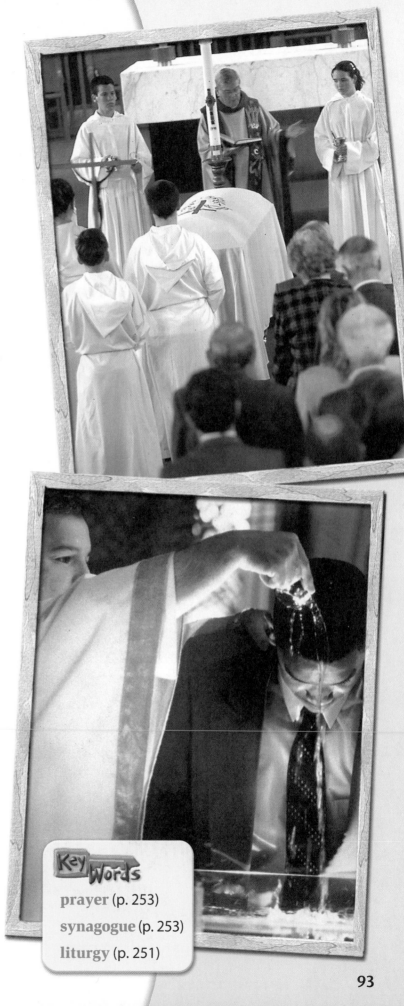

Key Words

prayer (p. 253)

synagogue (p. 253)

liturgy (p. 251)

There are different kinds of prayer.

Think of a time when something was so beautiful or amazing that it made you think "Wow!" That feeling can become a *prayer of praise*. "O God, you are wonderful!"

Think of a time when you passed a difficult test or when you felt better after being sick. You felt grateful that God had been so good to you. You said, "Thank you so much, O Lord!" This is a *prayer of thanksgiving*.

There are other times when we know that we have done wrong, when we have sinned. We ask God for forgiveness. This is a *prayer of petition*.

A prayer is often prayed before a meal. We pray to God to bless the gift of our food. This is a *prayer of blessing*.

We can ask God to help our families, friends, and all the people in the world. This is a *prayer of intercession*.

Look at the pictures on these pages. Below each write the type of prayer that might be said: praise, thanksgiving, petition, blessing, or intercession.

_____

The Church prays at all times.

Did you know that the Church is always at prayer? In one part of the world, children are beginning their school day by praying. Yet at the same time in another part of the world, children are saying their prayers before going to bed.

There are special prayers called the Liturgy of the Hours. These prayers are prayed seven different times during the day. So somewhere in the world, people are always praying the Liturgy of the Hours.

If we could travel around the world, we would be able to pray in different languages and in different ways. For example, in some countries, people pray by taking part in dances.

We would see other people praying by walking through the streets in processions. In some countries, we would see people praying at shrines set up along the roads. In other places, we would see people making journeys to holy places. These prayer-journeys are called **pilgrimages**.

The greatest prayer of the Church is the Mass. The Mass is the celebration of the Eucharist, the sacrament of the Body and Blood of Christ. It unites us all and leads us to live as Jesus' disciples.

WE RESPOND

In groups talk about some of the ways your parish prays. How do these ways help people to grow closer to God? Act out one of these ways for the rest of the class.

Key Word

pilgrimages (p. 252)

As Catholics...

We can pray with our bodies. We show respect for Jesus present in the Eucharist by genuflecting or bowing before the tabernacle. During Mass we pray by standing, kneeling, and sitting. At other times we pray with hands folded or with arms open wide. Sometimes people even pray by dancing!

How do you pray?

PROJECT

Show What you Know

Circle the answer to the clue in the letter box. Write the unused letters on the bottom blank lines. If you keep them in order, you will have a message you learned in this chapter.

1. Prayer journeys to a holy place.

2. Prayer that tells God he is wonderful.

3. A gathering place where Jewish People pray.

4. We ask God to do this before enjoying a meal.

5. Official public prayer of the Church.

6. Prayers asking for God's forgiveness.

7. Listening and talking to God.

```
T H E C P E T I T I O N
P I L G R I M A G E S H
U R C H A P R A Y S A T
A L L S Y N A G O G U E
T I M E E P R A I S E S
L I T U R G Y B L E S S
```

___ ___ ___ ___   ___ ___ ___ ___ ___ ___

___ ___ ___ ___ ___ ___ ___ ___

___ ___ ___ ___ ___ ___ ___ ___ ___ .

DISCIPLE

Pray
Learn
Celebrate
Share
Choose
Live

Question Corner

We can pray at any time and in any place. Fill out the survey about your favorite ways to pray.

My favorite place to pray _____

My favorite time to pray _____

My favorite prayer _____

What's the Word?

"Let my prayer be incense before you." (Psalm 141:2a)

Incense is resin from certain trees and spices. When sprinkled on hot coals it burns and makes smoke that rises up into the air. For the writer of this psalm, burning incense was an image of how our prayer rises to God.

↳ DISCIPLE CHALLENGE

• What prayer would you like to "rise to God"? Write it on the line.

_____

Fast Facts

At every Mass, we pray the *Prayer of the Faithful*. We pray for: Church leaders and the whole Church; world leaders and world situations; our neighborhoods; the sick; and those who have died. We can also offer our own personal prayers.

Take Home
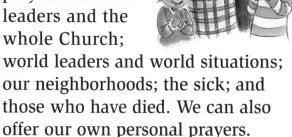

You learned that there are four forms of prayer. Think of a person in your family who is in need of prayer. Write two different kinds of prayer for this person.

Prayer of _____ for _____

_____

Prayer of _____ for _____

_____

CHAPTER TEST

Match the words in column A to the correct descriptions in column B.

A   B

1. pilgrimage   _____ gathering place where Jewish People pray and learn about God

2. prayer

_____ the greatest prayer of the Church

3. synagogue

_____ a prayer-journey to a holy place

4. liturgy

_____ the prayer Jesus taught his followers

5. the Lord's Prayer   _____ listening and talking to God

6. the Mass   _____ the official public prayer of the Church

Answer the following.

7–8. Write about some of the ways that Jesus prayed.

_____

_____

9–10. There are different kinds of prayer: praise, thanksgiving, petition, blessing, intercession. Choose two types and explain each.

_____

_____

WE GATHER

✝ **Leader:** Let us listen to the words of Jesus.

Reader: "I have called you friends. As I have loved you, so you also should love one another." (John 15:15; 13:34)

All: Thank you, Jesus, for calling us to be your friends and followers in the Church.

Reader: "For where two or three are gathered together in my name, there am I in the midst of them." (Matthew 18:20)

All: Thank you, Jesus, for our parish where we can gather in your name.

Reader: "Whatever you did for one of these least brothers of mine, you did for me." (Matthew 25:40)

All: Thank you, Jesus, for inviting us to do your work on earth. Help us to see you in all those in need. Amen.

☀ When does your whole family get together? Why?

WE BELIEVE
We belong to a parish.

A parish is like a family. A **parish** is a community of believers who worship and work together. It is made up of Catholics who usually live in the same neighborhood. It is part of a diocese which is led by a bishop.

The members of a parish share the same faith in Jesus Christ. Parish members:

- come together for the celebration of the Mass and other sacraments

- come together to pray, learn, and grow in faith

- work together to meet the needs of their parish

- welcome people who want to become members of the Church. These people learn from others about the Catholic faith. They prepare for the Sacraments of Baptism, Confirmation, and Eucharist.

You belong to a parish. In your parish there are many ways to live and grow as a Catholic.

 Draw or write about one time you took part in a parish activity.

Many people serve our parish.

Through our Baptism God calls each one of us. He calls us to do his work. This work is to bring the Good News of Jesus Christ to others. Helping in our parish is a way to serve God and the Church.

A **pastor** is the priest who leads the parish in worship, prayer, and teaching. His most important work is to lead the parish in the celebration of the Mass. The parish might have other priests who work with the pastor. They also lead the parish in the celebration of the sacraments and in parish activities.

Sometimes the parish has a deacon. A **deacon** is a man who is not a priest but has received the Sacrament of Holy Orders. He serves the parish by preaching, baptizing, and assisting the bishops and priests.

There are many ways of serving in your parish. These are called *ministries*. Some ministries are: catechist, director of youth services, director of social ministries, extraordinary minister of Holy Communion, director of music, altar server, and reader.

Can you name any other ministries? With a partner talk about how you and your family can help and serve your parish.

Key Words

parish (p. 252)
pastor (p. 252)
deacon (p. 250)

We are SAINT LUKE'S PARISH

Maria

Paul

Francis

Joanna

Our parish worships together.

Celebrations are an important part of parish life. The Church has always gathered to celebrate the life, Death, and Resurrection of Jesus. Participating in Mass is an important part of belonging to the Church.

Jesus said, "Where two or three are gathered together in my name, there am I in the midst of them." (Matthew 18:20) So when we gather as a parish, we are in the presence of Jesus. We gather to worship, to give thanks and praise to God.

Every time we celebrate Mass and the sacraments as a parish, we show our faith in Jesus. We show our love for him and for one another.

 Name one thing you enjoy about worshiping with your parish.

Our parish cares for others.

Our parish worship encourages us to help others. At the end of Mass, the priest or deacon sends us out to share God's love with others. He may say, "Go in peace." We answer, "Thanks be to God." But our real answer comes in our daily effort to help others.

We love and serve the Lord and others by:

- studying and learning more about our Catholic faith

- sharing the Good News

- sharing what we have—our money, our time, and our talents—with one another

- caring for those in need—the sick, the poor, and the hungry

- making peace with others, even those who hurt us

- working for justice by treating all people fairly and with respect

- protecting the rights of people who cannot stand up for themselves.

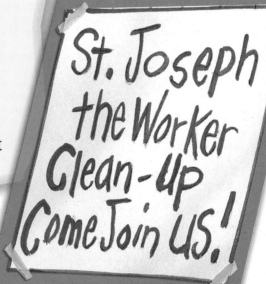

St. Joseph the Worker Clean-Up Come Join Us!

All these actions are not just nice things to do. They are ways to show that we are true followers of Jesus Christ and members of his Body, the Church.

WE RESPOND

What kinds of things take place in your parish? List some of these things using the letters below.

P _____
A _____
R _____
I _____
S _____
H _____

As Catholics...

Some parishes do not have priests to serve them. So the bishop of the diocese selects a *pastoral administrator* to serve the parish. This administrator leads parish activities. He or she guides the parish in religious education and prayer. However, the bishop always assigns a priest to celebrate Mass and the other sacraments at these parishes.

Do you know of any parishes with a pastoral administrator?

PROJECT

Show What you Know

Cross out every other letter to find each .
Then write its definition.

PSAIRAIPSAHR   _____

_____

POATSOTROPRA   _____

_____

DOECAECDOCNE   _____

_____

 **Pray Today**

Pray this prayer for your parish.

God, our Father, bless our parish.
Help us to welcome all who come to worship.

Jesus, be with us as we celebrate your life,
   Death, and Resurrection.

Holy Spirit, fill our parish with your love.
Help us to love one another in our parish
   and in our family.
Amen.

Now, pass it on!

Pray
Learn
Celebrate
Share
Choose
Live

Make it Happen

Design an award for a person who serves in your parish. It might be for the pastor, the deacon, or the school principal. On the award, write or draw one thing that this person does to bring the Good News of Jesus to others. Share your idea with your class.

Fast Facts

A recent survey found that there are over 64 million Catholics in the United States and approximately 18,479 parishes.

Take Home

During Mass we remember those who are sick. Next time you go to Mass with your family, listen for the names of those who need your prayers. Make a point of praying for these people during the next week.

CHAPTER TEST

Use the words in the box to complete the sentences.

1. A _____ is a community of believers who worship and work together.

2. The priest who leads the parish is called the _____.

3. A man who is not a priest but has received the Sacrament of

   Holy Orders is a _____.

| deacon |
| parish |
| pastor |

Write T if the statement is True. Write F if the sentence is false.

4. _____ When we gather as a parish, we are in the presence of Jesus.

5. _____ There are only a few ways of serving in a parish.

6. _____ One way a deacon serves the Church is by baptizing people.

Answer the following.

7–8. Write a few of the ministries of your parish.

_____

_____

9–10. Write two or three ways you can love and serve the Lord and
      one another.

_____

_____

_____

God Calls Us to Holiness

WE GATHER

✝ **Leader:** Let us listen to the Word of God.

Reader: A reading from the first Letter of Saint John

"Beloved, if God so loved us, we also must love one another. No one has ever seen God. Yet, if we love one another, God remains in us, and his love is brought to perfection in us." (1 John 4:11, 12)

The word of the Lord.

All: Thanks be to God.

🎵 Only a Shadow

The love we have for you, O Lord,
Is only a shadow of your love for us;
Only a shadow of your love for us;
Your deep abiding love.

Our lives are in your hands,
Our lives are in your hands.
Our love for you will grow, O Lord;
Your light in us will shine.
Your light in us will shine
'Til we meet face to face.

☀ What would you say if someone asked you, "What do you want to be when you grow up?"

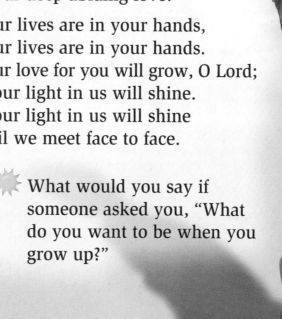

WE BELIEVE

God calls each of us.

In Baptism God calls all of us to love and to serve him. This is the mission we share as members of the Church. Our mission is to learn from Jesus and to continue his work in the world. We are called to show others who Jesus is so they will love and follow him, too.

A **vocation** is God's call to serve him in a certain way. Each baptized person has a vocation to love and serve God. There are specific ways to follow our vocation: as single or married people, religious brothers or sisters, or priests or deacons.

None of us lives our vocation alone. We live it as a member of the Church.

With a partner talk about people in your parish who follow their vocations to serve God. Give some examples of how they do this.

God calls everyone to be holy.

Most Catholics live out their vocation as laypeople. **Laypeople** are baptized members of the Church who share in the mission to bring the Good News of Christ to the world.

Some laypeople are called to the vocation of married life. A husband and wife show Jesus to the world by the love that unites them. One important way they live out their vocations is by teaching their family to pray and to follow Jesus Christ.

Some laypeople live their vocation as single people in the world. They, too, answer God's call by living their lives as Jesus did. They use their time and talents to serve others.

Key Words

vocation (p. 253)

laypeople (p. 251)

God calls all people to holiness. Our holiness comes from sharing God's life. To live a life of holiness means to share the Good News of Jesus and help to build up God's Kingdom. We do this when we:

- tell others in our parish, our school, and our workplace about Jesus

- treat others as Jesus did

- care for those in need

- help others to know that God's life and love are alive in the world.

Look at the pictures. How is each person following his or her vocation?

Draw a way you follow God's call right now.

God calls some men to be priests or deacons.

Some men are called to serve God and the Church as priests or permanent deacons. When a man follows this call, he accepts a special ministry within the Church. He is ordained as a priest or deacon by a bishop.

In the Sacrament of Holy Orders, the bishop lays his hands on the head of the man to be ordained. The bishop asks the Holy Spirit to strengthen the new priest or deacon in his ministry.

Priests have a very important role in the Church. They preach the message of Jesus and help us to live our faith. Priests lead us in the celebration of the Mass and the sacraments. They promise not to marry. This allows them to share God's love with all people and to go wherever the bishop sends them.

Permanent deacons are single or married men ordained to a special ministry of service—preaching, baptizing, and serving the Church.

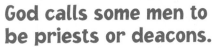 How have the priests or deacons in your parish helped you learn about Jesus?

Ask God to help them to continue their work in the Church.

God calls some people to religious life.

Some Church members follow Jesus Christ in the religious life. They are priests, brothers, or sisters who belong to religious communities. They share their lives with God and others in a special way.

As members of their religious communities they make **vows**, or promises to God. The vows usually are chastity, poverty, and obedience. Those in religious life promise to:

• live a life of loving service to the Church and their religious community. By not marrying they can devote themselves to sharing God's love with all people.

- live simply as Jesus did and own no personal property.

- promise to listen carefully to God's direction in their lives and to go wherever their religious community sends them to do God's work.

Those in religious life serve the Church in many different ways. Some live alone; others live in community. Some live apart from the world so they can pray all the time. Others combine prayer with a life of service as teachers, social workers, missionaries, doctors, and nurses.

vows (p. 253)

As Catholics...

There are two different ways of serving in the priestly life. Diocesan priests serve in a diocese, usually in a parish.

Priests in religious communities, such as the Franciscans and the Jesuits, serve wherever their community needs them. They might be missionaries, teachers, doctors, or writers. But whatever their work, their vocation is to serve God through their priesthood.

Are the priests in your parish diocesan priests? or are they in a religious community?

WE RESPOND

The Church needs the help and support of people in every vocation. Each vocation is important for the growth of the Church.

Write a prayer asking God to help all Church members in their vocations.

_____

_____

PROJECT

Show What you Know

Match the symbol with its letter to find the Key Word that completes the sentence.

✺	♣	★	⦸	♥	⊕	✠	❉	◆	⊛	☘	◎	✤
A	C	E	I	L	N	O	P	S	T	V	W	Y

1. A ____ ____ ____ ____ ____ ____ ____ ____ is God's call to serve him in a
   ☘ ✠ ♣ ✺ ⊛ ⦸ ✠ ⊕

   certain way.

2. ____ ____ ____ ____ ____ ____ ____ ____ ____ are baptized members of the
   ♥ ✺ ✤ ❉ ★ ✠ ❉ ♥ ★

   Church who share in the mission to bring the Good News of Christ to the world.

3. Members of religious communities make ____ ____ ____ ____, or promises
   ☘ ✠ ◎ ◆

   to God.

What Would you do?

Which of the following would you do to try to live a life of holiness? Circle **Yes** or **No**.

- Invite a new student to eat lunch with you. **Yes** **No**
- Ignore your mother when she tells you to clean your room. **Yes** **No**
- Pray for children and their families who are homeless. **Yes** **No**
- Get upset when a friend wants to play a different game. **Yes** **No**

DISCIPLE

Pray
Learn
Celebrate
Share
Choose
Live

Saint Stories

The saints are examples of holiness. Martin de Porres was born in Lima, Peru in 1579. During his childhood he was not always treated with respect. But he learned how to treat others with respect.

When he grew up, Martin became a religious brother. He spent each day caring for poor children and for the sick and homeless. Learn more examples of holiness by visiting *Lives of the Saints* at www.webelieveweb.com.

More *to* Explore

No matter our vocation, we can all be missionaries. Missionaries bring the Good News of Jesus out into the world. Glenmary Home Missioners serve people in small-town and rural areas of the United States. Find out more about the Glenmary Home Missioners by visiting www.glenmary.org.

↳ **DISCIPLE CHALLENGE** Write one thing you discover in your search.

Take Home

Take a holiness survey with your family. Ask each member what they do in a work day.

How do they serve God through their work?

CHAPTER TEST

Write T if the sentence is true. Write F if the sentence is false.

1. _____ In Baptism God calls all people to love and serve him.

2. _____ Laypeople are baptized members of the Church who share in the mission to bring the Good News of Christ to the world.

3. _____ Those in religious life make vows, or promises to God.

4. _____ Bishops ordain priests and deacons through the Sacrament of Confirmation.

5. _____ God calls only some people to holiness.

6. _____ The Church needs the help and support of people in every vocation.

Answer the following.

7–8. Write two promises members of religious communities make to God.

_____

_____

9–10. Write two ways we live a life of holiness.

_____

_____

"Prepare the way of the Lord, make straight his paths."

Luke 3:4

SEASONAL

CHAPTER 13

This chapter prepares us to celebrate the season of Advent.

The season of Advent helps us prepare for the coming of the Son of God.

WE GATHER

🎵 **Prepare the Way**

Prepare the way
for the coming of God.
Make a straight path
for the coming of God.

WE BELIEVE

The word *Advent* means "coming." Each year during Advent we prepare to celebrate the first coming of the Son of God. We prepare to celebrate the birth of Jesus Christ at Christmas.

During Advent, we rejoice that Jesus is our Savior. He is the Son of God sent to save us from sin. We remember that God's people waited many, many years for the Savior to come. During those years of waiting, God spoke to his people through the prophets. The prophets told the people to prepare for the Savior.

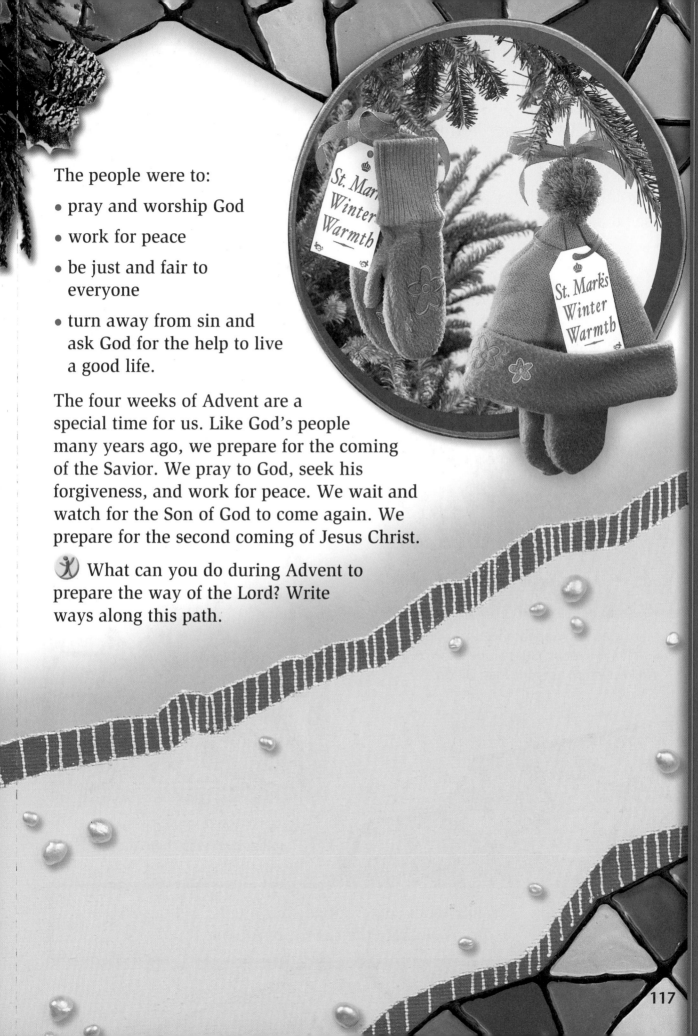

The people were to:

- pray and worship God

- work for peace

- be just and fair to everyone

- turn away from sin and ask God for the help to live a good life.

The four weeks of Advent are a special time for us. Like God's people many years ago, we prepare for the coming of the Savior. We pray to God, seek his forgiveness, and work for peace. We wait and watch for the Son of God to come again. We prepare for the second coming of Jesus Christ.

What can you do during Advent to prepare the way of the Lord? Write ways along this path.

WE RESPOND

The Church honors saints all year long. Here are some saints that we honor during Advent. They help us to rejoice in the coming of the Lord. Their lives help us to see that the Lord is near.

The people of Sweden were suffering from hunger. They prayed to Saint Lucy. They soon received help.

Mary made an appearance to a poor man who lived in Guadalupe, Mexico. We know him as Saint Juan Diego.

Saint Nicholas helped poor families by giving them money.

Talk about some things your family and parish do to celebrate the season of Advent.

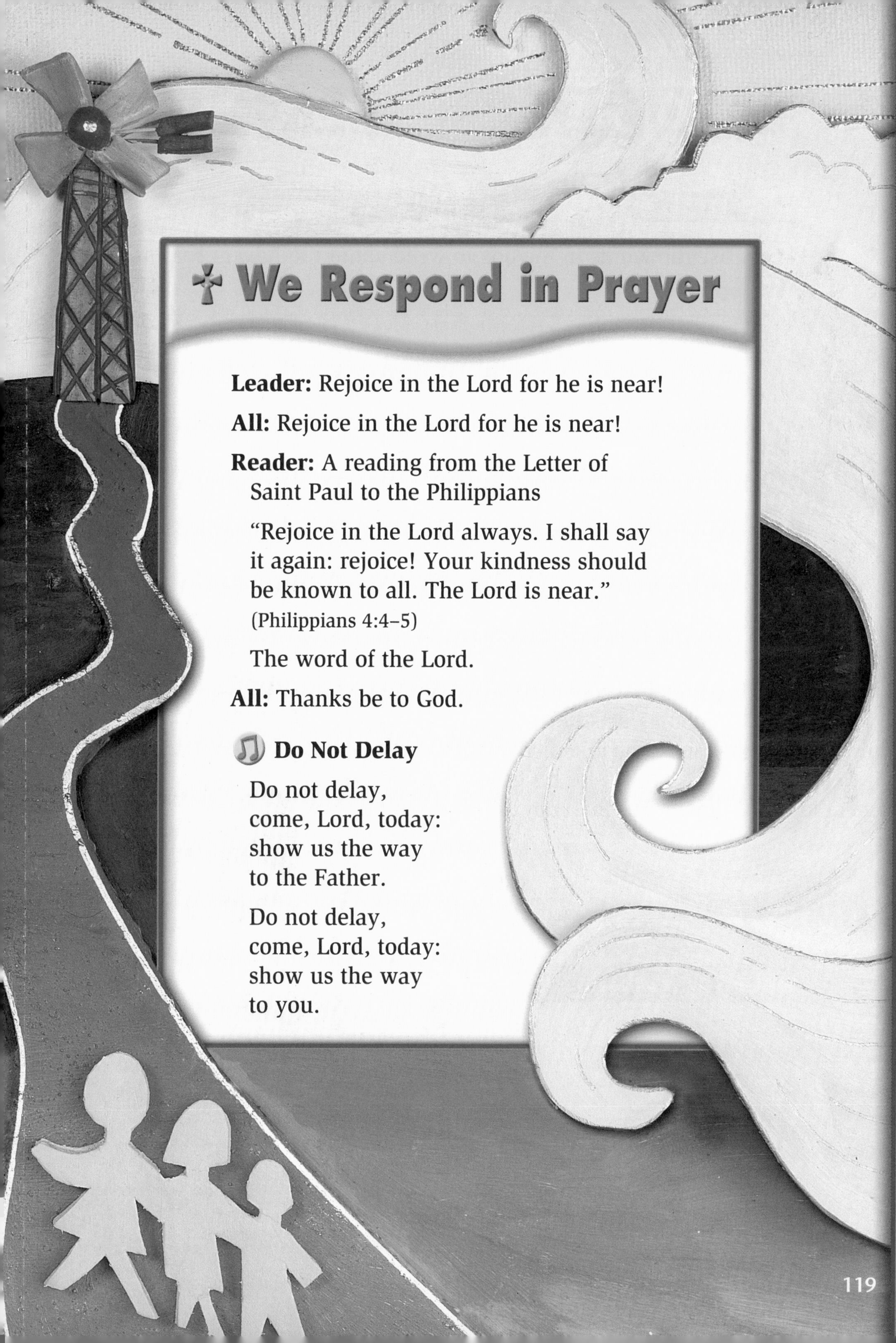

✝ We Respond in Prayer

Leader: Rejoice in the Lord for he is near!

All: Rejoice in the Lord for he is near!

Reader: A reading from the Letter of Saint Paul to the Philippians

"Rejoice in the Lord always. I shall say it again: rejoice! Your kindness should be known to all. The Lord is near."
(Philippians 4:4–5)

The word of the Lord.

All: Thanks be to God.

🎵 **Do Not Delay**

Do not delay,
come, Lord, today:
show us the way
to the Father.

Do not delay,
come, Lord, today:
show us the way
to you.

PROJECT DISCIPLE

Show What *you* Know

Use the words in the box to write about the Advent season.

| Advent |
| prepare |
| Savior |
| prophets |
| pray |
| worship |

_____

_____

_____

_____

_____

Saint Stories

Saint Nicholas was bishop of Myra, a city located in a country that is now Turkey. Nicholas was born into a wealthy family but used the money he inherited to assist those who were poor. He was known for his generosity and for his great love of children. His feast day is December 6th.

What Would *you* do?

During Advent I will...	
Week 1	
Week 2	
Week 3	
Week 4	

Take Home

Talk with your family about ways to prepare during the four weeks of Advent. Make a plan.

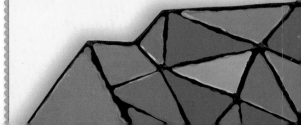

"Today is born our Savior, Christ the Lord!"
Responsorial Psalm, Christmas Mass at Midnight

SEASONAL

CHAPTER 14

This chapter addresses the entire Christmas season.

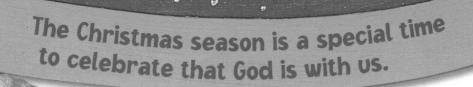
The Christmas season is a special time to celebrate that God is with us.

WE GATHER

Have you ever waited for someone?
How did you feel when that person arrived?
What did you do to celebrate?

WE BELIEVE

During the season of Christmas we celebrate that the wait is over. The Savior that God's people had waited for has come. The Son of God became one of us to save us. Jesus is the Son of God who lived among us.

Luke 2:1–12

During the time of Mary and Joseph, the emperor made a new rule. All the people of the whole world had to be counted. All men had to go to the town of their father's family. They had to sign a list and be counted.

Joseph was from Bethlehem, the city of David. So he had to go to Bethlehem with Mary.

"While they were there, the time came for her to have her child, and she gave birth to her firstborn son. She wrapped him in swaddling clothes and laid him in a manger, because there was no room for them in the inn." (Luke 2:6–7)

There were shepherds in the fields nearby. The angel of the Lord came to them and said:

"Do not be afraid; for behold, I proclaim to you good news of great joy that will be for all the people. For today in the city of David a savior has been born for you who is Messiah and Lord. You will find an infant wrapped in swaddling clothes and lying in a manger." (Luke 2:10–12)

Jesus is our Lord and Messiah. During Advent and Christmas we hear Jesus called Emmanuel. The name *Emmanuel* means "God with us." This is what we are celebrating during Christmas: God is with us today, now, and forever.

 One way we share the joy of Christmas is through music. Write your own song to tell others the Good News that Jesus is with us. Use a tune you know or make up one of your own.

_____

_____

_____

The Christmas season is a season of celebration. The Church celebrates many important feasts during this time.

December 25	Christmas
First Sunday after Christmas...........................	Holy Family
Second Sunday after Christmas....................	Epiphany
Third Sunday after Christmas.......................	The Baptism of the Lord
December 26	Saint Stephen
December 27	Saint John the Apostle
December 28	The Holy Innocents
December 29	Saint Thomas Becket
January 1..	Mary, the Mother of God
January 4..	Saint Elizabeth Ann Seton
January 5..	Saint John Neumann

WE RESPOND

Draw a picture to show one way your parish celebrates during the Christmas season.

✝ We Respond in Prayer

Leader: We thank you, God, for the lives of your holy people. Be with us as we ask their prayers for us.

All: Blessed be God for ever.

Reader: Saint Stephen was a deacon. He was the first to give his life for his faith in Jesus.

Saint Stephen,

All: Pray for us.

Reader: Jesus chose John to be an Apostle. Saint John was the writer of one of the four Gospels. He wrote that God is love.

Saint John,

All: Pray for us.

Reader: King Herod did not want Jesus the Savior to live. He ordered all the baby boys two years of age and under to be killed! We call them the Holy Innocents. Their lives remind us of God's great gift of life.

Holy Innocents,

All: Pray for us.

Leader: Jesus shares God's gift of life with each of us. Praise God!

All: Blessed be God for ever.

PROJECT DISCIPLE

Celebrate!

Many feast days are celebrated during the Christmas season. Look at the chart on page 124 to help you match the name of the feast with the date it is celebrated.

1. Holy Innocents _____ December 25

2. Christmas _____ December 26

3. Mary, Mother of God _____ December 27

4. Saint John the Apostle _____ December 28

5. Saint Elizabeth Ann Seton _____ January 1

6. Saint Stephen _____ January 4

Picture This

What does the name *Emmanuel* mean? Design a Christmas ornament to tell others of its meaning.

Take Home

On the first Sunday after Christmas, the Church celebrates the Feast of the Holy Family. Make this a special day for your family.

UNIT TEST

Match the words in column A to the correct descriptions in column B.

A   B

1. vocation   _____ promise to God

2. prayer   _____ listening and talking to God

3. Apostles' Creed   _____ the official public prayer of the Church

4. vow   _____ God's call to serve him in a certain way

5. liturgy   _____ Christian statement of beliefs

Write T if the sentence is true. Write F if the sentence is false.

6. _____ Catholic social teaching tells us that we have a responsibility to share the good things of the world.

7. _____ The bishops of the Church are the successors of the Apostles.

8. _____ The Lord's Prayer is also called Our Prayer.

9. _____ One mark of the Church is that it is *catholic*, which means "universal."

10. _____ Priests, sisters, and brothers who belong to religious communities make vows of poverty, chastity, and justice.

continued on next page   **127**

Write sentences to answer the questions.

11. What is the role of the pastor of a parish?

_____

_____

12. What are some of the ways laypeople live out their vocation?

_____

_____

13. Why is the Mass the greatest prayer of the Church?

_____

_____

14. What is one truth we state we believe in when we pray the Apostles' Creed?

_____

_____

15. What is one way we can show we are true followers of Jesus Christ and members of the Church?

_____

_____

The Church Leads Us in Worship

UNIT
3

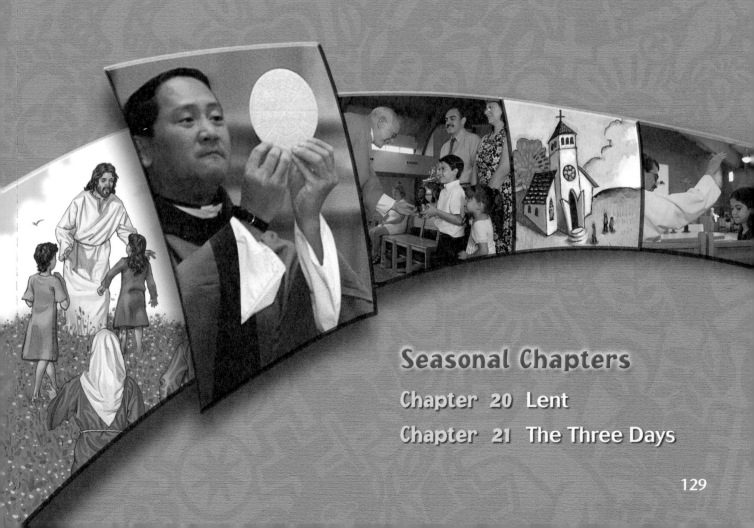

Seasonal Chapters

Pray
Learn
Celebrate
Share
Choose
Live

PROJECT DISCIPLE

DEAR FAMILY

In Unit 3 your child will grow as a disciple of Jesus by:

- celebrating the Seven Sacraments that Jesus gave us
- understanding that the Mass is both a sacrifice and a meal
- gathering with the parish community to worship God at Mass and to be strengthened by Holy Communion to serve others
- making choices that show love for God and others, and seeking God's forgiveness for sin in the Sacrament of Penance
- learning that the Church offers healing in Jesus' name through the Sacrament of the Anointing of the Sick.

What's the Word?

Chapter 15 includes a description about the Anointing of the Sick. To learn about Jesus' care of the sick, read together Luke 5:17–25. Talk about what happened to the man and how his friends made sure he got to see Jesus. How can your family help to bring others to Jesus? What will you do this week?

Show That You Care

Unit 3 reviews the Seven Sacraments. Does your family know someone who will be receiving one of the sacraments this year? Is there a friend or relative who will be baptized or celebrate Matrimony? Is anyone you know receiving First Holy Communion? Offer your prayers and encouragement to these people and for all who receive the sacraments this year.

Reality Check

"The family is the 'domestic church' where God's children learn to pray 'as the Church' and to persevere in prayer."
(*Catechism of the Catholic Church, 2685*)

Picture This

Look at the photos of the Sacrament of Penance and Reconciliation on pages 158–159. Remind your child that God always forgives us if we are truly sorry and that God asks us to forgive those who hurt us, too. How does your family express sorrow and forgiveness to each other?

Celebrate!

At the celebration of the Eucharist, the Church gives thanks to God. As a family, talk about all of the things for which you are thankful. Remember all of these things at the celebration of the Eucharist this Sunday.

Take Home

Be ready for:

Chapter 15: Finding sacramentals at your home

Chapter 16: Donating money at Mass

Chapter 17: Reflecting on Sunday's readings

Chapter 18: Rating TV programs

Chapter 19: Remembering the dead

We Celebrate the Sacraments

WE GATHER

✝ **Leader:** God loves us very much. Let us thank God for all the ways he shows his love for us. Let us thank God for sending his Son.

Reader: "For God so loved the world that he gave his only Son, so that everyone who believes in him might not perish but might have eternal life."(John 3:16)

All: Thank you, God, for giving us your Son, Jesus. Amen.

🎵 **Jesus Is with Us**

Jesus is with us today,
beside us to guide us today.
Jesus teaches us, Jesus heals us,
for we are his Church;
we are his chosen;
we are the children of God.

☀ What are some signs that you see in your neighborhood? Tell why each one is important.

131

WE BELIEVE

The Church celebrates the sacraments.

Every day we can see all kinds of signs. A sign stands for or tells us about something. A sign can be something we see or something we do.

Jesus often pointed to ordinary things to help us to learn more about God. He spoke about birds, wheat, and even wildflowers as signs of God's love. Jesus' actions were signs of God's love, too. He held children in his arms. He touched people and healed them. He comforted sinners and forgave them.

The Church celebrates seven special signs. We call these signs *sacraments*. A **sacrament** is a special sign given to us by Jesus through which we share in God's life and love. The Seven Sacraments are Baptism, Confirmation, Eucharist, Penance and Reconciliation, Anointing of the Sick, Holy Orders, and Matrimony.

Through the power of the Holy Spirit, we receive and celebrate God's own life and love in the sacraments. Our share in God's life and love is called **grace**. Through the power of grace, we grow in holiness. The sacraments help us to live as Jesus' disciples.

List the sacraments you have received.

_____

_____

_____

As Catholics...

Sacramentals are blessings, actions, and special objects given to us by the Church. They help us to respond to the grace we receive in the sacraments. Blessings of people, places, and food are sacramentals. Actions such as making the Sign of the Cross and the sprinkling of holy water are sacramentals. Some objects that are sacramentals are statues, medals, rosaries, candles, and crucifixes.

Name a sacramental that is part of your life at home.

Baptism, Confirmation, and Eucharist are the Sacraments of Christian Initiation.

We are joined to Jesus and the Church through the Sacraments of Christian Initiation: Baptism, Confirmation, and Eucharist. Another word for *initiation* is *beginning*. Through the Sacraments of Christian Initiation, a new life of grace begins in us.

In Baptism the Church welcomes us. We become children of God and members of the Church. Each of us is born with Original Sin, the first sin committed by the first human beings. Through Baptism God frees us from Original Sin and forgives any sins we may have committed. God fills us with grace, his life and love.

In Confirmation we are sealed with the Gift of the Holy Spirit. The Holy Spirit gives us strength and courage to live as disciples of Jesus.

In the Eucharist we praise and thank God the Father for sending his Son, Jesus. We receive Jesus' Body and Blood in Holy Communion. We grow closer to Jesus and all the members of the Church.

Key Words

sacrament (p. 253)

grace (p. 251)

Sacraments of Christian Initiation (p. 253)

Original Sin (p. 252)

In groups talk about how your parish celebrates the Sacraments of Christian Initiation.

Penance and Reconciliation and Anointing of the Sick are Sacraments of Healing.

During his ministry Jesus healed many people. Sometimes he did this when he cured them of their sicknesses. At other times Jesus forgave people their sins.

Jesus gave the Church the power to continue his healing work. The Church does this especially through two sacraments: Penance and Reconciliation and Anointing of the Sick. These sacraments are called Sacraments of Healing.

In the Sacrament of Penance and Reconciliation, we confess our sins to the priest and promise to do better. In the name of God, the priest forgives our sins. Our relationship with God and others is healed.

In the Sacrament of the Anointing of the Sick, the priest lays his hands on the sick. He blesses them with holy oil and prays for their health. They are strengthened in their faith and sometimes their bodies are healed. They receive the peace of Christ.

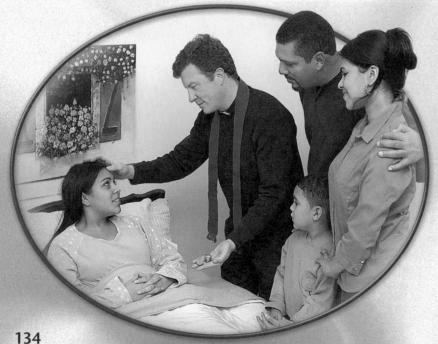

✴ Think about someone you need to forgive or someone you know who is sick. What can you do to show them your love and care?

Holy Orders and Matrimony are Sacraments of Service to others.

Through Baptism God calls each one of us to be a sign of his love to others. We each have a vocation to serve God and the Church. The Church celebrates two sacraments that are special signs of service: Holy Orders and Matrimony.

In the Sacrament of Holy Orders, baptized men are ordained to serve the Church as deacons, priests, and bishops. This sacrament gives them the grace to live out their vocation of service in the Church.

Bishops serve the Church by leading a larger community of faith called a diocese. They lead their dioceses in service, teaching, prayer, and sacraments. Under their guidance, priests also carry on the ministry of Jesus.

Priests usually serve in parishes. They lead the celebration of the sacraments, guide the people they serve, and reach out to those who are in need. Some priests teach in schools.

Along with the bishop and priests, deacons are ordained to serve their dioceses. Deacons do many things to help in their parish worship. They also have a special responsibility to serve those who are in need.

In the Sacrament of Matrimony, or Marriage, the love of a man and woman is blessed. They are united in the love of Christ. The husband and wife receive the grace to help them to be faithful to each other. The sacrament also helps the couple to share God's love with their family. They grow in holiness as they serve the Church together.

WE RESPOND

Draw or write how you and your friends join in the celebration of the sacraments.

Pray
Learn
Celebrate
Share
Choose
Live

PROJECT

Show What *you* Know

Emma's brother hit the delete key after Emma worked on her
 Key Word definitions. Use the words in the box to help Emma
restore her work.

A _____ is a special _____ given to us by

_____ through which we share in God's life and love.

_____ is our share in God's _____

and _____.

Baptism, Confirmation, and Eucharist are the Sacraments

of _____.

_____ is the first sin committed by the first
human beings.

life
Christian Initiation
sacrament
Original Sin
Jesus
love
grace
sign

What's *the* Word?

*"At sunset, all who had people sick with
various diseases brought them to [Jesus].
He laid his hands on each of them and
cured them."* (Luke 4:40)

- Why did the people bring their sick loved

  ones to Jesus? _____

  _____

- What did Jesus do when he cured people?

  _____

Pray
Learn
Celebrate
Share
Choose
Live

More to Explore

In 1980, four American Catholic women, Sister Ita Ford, Sister Maura Clarke, Sister Dorothy Kazel, and Jean Donovan were killed in El Salvador. They died as they had lived, serving God and the Church.

↳ DISCIPLE CHALLENGE A *martyr* is someone who dies for his or her faith. Many martyrs have been declared saints by the Church. Read about some on *Lives of the Saints* at www.webelieveweb.com.

Celebrate!

In the Sacrament of Matrimony, a man and a woman are united in the love of Christ. Think of a married couple that you know. Write some ways that they share God's love with their own family and with others.

_____

_____

Pray Today

Complete the following prayer.

Jesus, you gave us the sacraments as signs that we share in God's life and love. Help me to be a sign of God's love in today's world. Help me to

_____

_____ **Now, pass it on!**

Take Home

Have you and your family made a prayer space in your home? If so, have you included some sacramentals? (a statue, medals, rosary, crucifix)

What sacramentals are in your prayer space?

_____

Why are they special to your family?

_____

CHAPTER TEST

Fill in the circle beside the correct answer.

1. The Sacraments of Christian Initiation are _____, Confirmation, and Eucharist.

   ○ Baptism   ○ Matrimony

2. The Sacraments of Healing are _____ and Anointing of the Sick.

   ○ Baptism   ○ Penance and Reconciliation

3. The Sacraments of Service to others are Holy Orders and _____.

   ○ Penance and Reconciliation   ○ Matrimony

4. In Baptism we are freed from _____.

   ○ grace   ○ Original Sin

Write T if the sentence is true. Write F if the sentence is false.

5. _____ Jesus did not give any one the power to continue his healing work.

6. _____ Grace is our share in God's life and love.

7. _____ In Confirmation we are sealed with the Gift of the Holy Spirit.

8. _____ There are twelve sacraments.

Answer the following.

9. Write two ways Jesus healed people.

   _____

   _____

10. Write two things that happen in the Sacrament of Baptism.

   _____

   _____

Celebrating Eucharist: The Mass

16

WE GATHER

✝ **Leader:** Everything good that we have is God's gift to us. Think quietly about what God has given you.

Reader: "Give thanks to the LORD, who is good, whose love endures forever."
(Psalm 106:1)

All: We thank you, O God!

Reader: "You are my God, I give you thanks; my God, I offer you praise."
(Psalm 118:28)

All: We thank you, O God!

☀ Many people celebrate special times with special meals. When have you and your family done this? What made the celebration special for you?

WE BELIEVE

Jesus celebrated Passover and the Last Supper.

Throughout their history, Jewish people have celebrated important events with special meals. On the feast of Passover, the Jewish people celebrate their freedom from slavery in Egypt. They remember that God "passed over" the houses of his people, saving them. They remember that God protected them from the suffering that came to Egypt.

On the night before he died, Jesus celebrated the Passover meal with his disciples in a new way. This meal that Jesus celebrated is called the *Last Supper.*

 Matthew 26:26–28

While Jesus and his disciples ate, Jesus took bread and blessed it. He then broke it and gave it to his disciples saying, "Take and eat; this is my body." (Matthew 26:26) Then Jesus took a cup of wine and gave thanks. He gave the cup to his disciples saying, "Drink from it, all of you, for this is my blood." (Matthew 26:27, 28)

At the Last Supper Jesus told his disciples to bless and break bread in his memory. He gave us the Eucharist. The Eucharist is the sacrament of Jesus' Body and Blood. At each celebration of the Eucharist, the Church follows Jesus' command to "Do this in memory of me." (Luke 22:19)

The word *eucharist* means "to give thanks." At the celebration of the Eucharist, the Church gives thanks for all that God gives us.

Write what you can thank God for at the celebration of the Eucharist.

_____

_____

The Mass is a sacrifice and a meal.

The greatest gift God has given to us is his Son, Jesus. Jesus' greatest gift is giving up his life for us. The Church remembers Jesus' Death and Resurrection at the Eucharist.

The celebration of the Eucharist is also called the **Mass**. The Mass is a sacrifice. A **sacrifice** is a gift offered to God by a priest in the name of all the people. Jesus offered the greatest sacrifice of all–his own body and blood on the cross. By his sacrifice Jesus reconciles us with God and saves us from sin.

Key Words

Passover (p. 252)

Eucharist (p. 251)

Mass (p. 252)

sacrifice (p. 253)

The Mass is also a meal. We remember what Jesus did at the Last Supper. He changed bread and wine into his Body and Blood. At Mass we receive his Body and Blood in Holy Communion. We are strengthened to live out our faith.

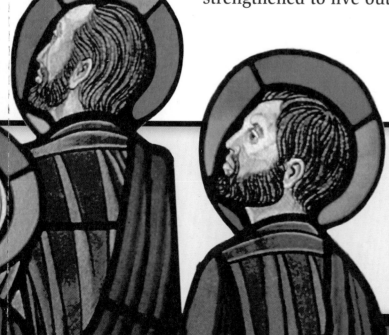

What could you tell a younger child about what the Mass is? Act it out with a partner.

We take part in the Mass.

The Mass is a celebration. It is the Church's great prayer of thanksgiving and praise. It is important that each of us participate in the celebration.

We gather as the assembly. The **assembly** is the people gathered to worship in the name of Jesus Christ.

We can all:

- pray the responses
- sing praise to God
- listen to the readings and the homily
- pray for needs of the community
- offer the sign of peace to others
- receive Holy Communion.

The priest who leads us at the Mass is called the *celebrant*. Many parishes have deacons who serve at the Mass. Greeters and ushers welcome us and help us to find seats. During the Mass they collect our donations. Altar servers help the priest before, during, and after Mass.

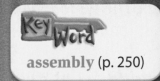

Key Word

assembly (p. 250)

As Catholics...

Altar servers are men, women, boys, and girls who serve at the altar. They light the altar candles. They lead the entrance procession at the beginning of Mass. They may help the priest and deacon receive the gifts of bread and wine. They lead everyone out of church at the end of Mass.

Find out how boys and girls can become altar servers.

The musicians and choir lead us in singing. The reader proclaims passages from Scripture. Members of the assembly present the gifts of bread and wine. Extraordinary ministers of Holy Communion can help the priest give us Holy Communion.

How do you take part in the Mass? Talk about ways you can encourage others to participate in Mass.

We celebrate Mass each week.

Sunday is our great holy day. It is the day on which Jesus Christ rose from the dead. The Resurrection of Jesus took place on "the first day of the week." (Matthew 28:1)

In our parishes we come together at Mass each Sunday or Saturday evening. We give praise and thanks to God. Celebrating the Eucharist together is the center of Catholic life. That is why the Church requires all Catholics to take part in the weekly celebration of the Mass. We are also required to participate in Mass on special feasts called *holy days of obligation*.

There are many other important feast days in the Church. One of these is the Feast of Our Lady of Guadalupe, which we celebrate on December 12. On these feasts and on every day of the year, we can take part in the Eucharist.

WE RESPOND

Send a message inviting people in your parish to take part in the Mass.

Holy Days of Obligation

Solemnity of Mary, Mother of God
(January 1)

Ascension
(when celebrated on Thursday during the Easter season)*

Assumption of Mary
(August 15)

All Saints' Day
(November 1)

Immaculate Conception
(December 8)

Christmas
(December 25)

*(Some dioceses celebrate the Ascension on the following Sunday.)

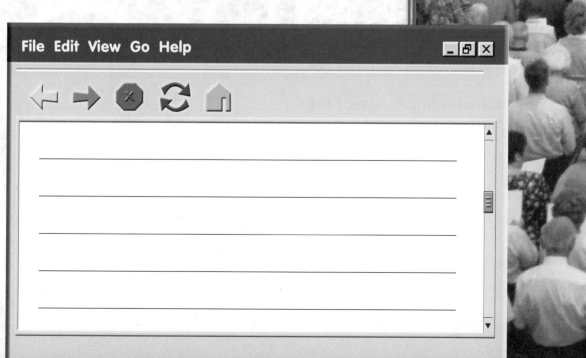

File   Edit   View   Go   Help

PROJECT

Pray
Learn
Celebrate
Share
Choose
Live

Show What *you* Know

Use the clues to help you unscramble the **Key Words**.

Clue	Scrambled Key Word	Your Answer
celebration of the Eucharist	SAMS	
people gathered to worship in the name of Jesus Christ	BYMAELSS	
the Jewish feast celebrating freedom from slavery in Egypt	ASPSEVOR	
the sacrament of Jesus' Body and Blood	ATIHSUREC	
a gift offered to God by a priest in the name of all the people	SCFCEIRAI	

Pray Today

The word *eucharist* means "to give thanks." Fill in the blanks. Then offer a prayer to thank God for each of these people.

♡ Someone who loves me _____

✎ Someone who teaches me about my faith _____

☺ Someone who makes me laugh _____

☂ Someone who takes care of me _____

Fast Facts

Campaign for Human Development helps people who are living in poverty. Once a year, parishes take up a special collection at Mass for this important work. Visit www.usccb.org/cchd/.

Pray
Learn
Celebrate
Share
Choose
Live

Saint Stories

Pope Saint Pius X was pope from 1903 to 1914. He was devoted to the Eucharist. Before he became pope, young children were not allowed to receive Holy Communion. Pius X changed that by saying children could receive the Eucharist when they understood the meaning of the sacrament. He urged all Catholics to receive Holy Communion more often.

↘ **DISCIPLE CHALLENGE** Find out more about this pope on *Lives of the Saints* at **www.webelieveweb.com**.

• When did Pope Pius X become a saint? _____

• When is his feast day? _____

What's *the* Word?

In the Old Testament, God said to the Jewish People:

"Remember to keep holy the sabbath day. Six days you may labor and do all your work, but the seventh day is the sabbath of the Lord, your God" (Exodus 20:8–10).

One way we can keep the Lord's Day holy is to enjoy being with our family. What will your family do together next Sunday?

_____

_____

_____

Take Home

Your family can follow Jesus by sharing what you have with your parish and others in need. This Sunday, as you give to the collection at Mass, pray that it will make a difference.

Match the words in column A to the correct descriptions in column B.

A	B

A

B

1. assembly

_____ feast celebrating freedom from slavery in Egypt

2. sacrifice

_____ celebration of the Eucharist

3. Passover

_____ a gift offered to God by a priest in the name of all the people

4. the Mass

_____ the people gathered to worship God in the name of Jesus Christ

Complete the sentences.

5. The Mass is a _____ and a sacrifice.

6. The _____ is the meal that Jesus celebrated with his disciples on the night before he died.

7. The _____ is the sacrament of Jesus' Body and Blood.

8. The word _eucharist_ means "_____."

Write sentences to answer the questions.

9. How does the assembly take part in the celebration of Mass?

_____

10. Why do Catholics gather for Mass each Sunday or Saturday evening?

_____

We Worship at Mass

WE GATHER

✝ **Leader:** Let us pray by singing.

🎵 **Jesus, We Believe in You**

Chorus
> Jesus, we believe in you;
> we believe that you are with us.
> Jesus, we believe in you;
> we believe that you are here.

> We believe that you are present with us here
> as we gather in your name. (Chorus)

> We believe that you are with us at all times,
> and your love will guide our way. (Chorus)

Leader: Jesus, thank you for your presence in our lives,

All: today and always. Amen.

☀ What are some things you get ready for?
How do you prepare?

WE BELIEVE

We gather to praise God.

The first part of the Mass is called the Introductory Rites. In the Introductory Rites we become one as we prepare to listen to God's Word and to celebrate the Eucharist.

We gather together as members of the Church, the Body of Christ. We sing an opening song of praise to God. Then the priest welcomes us as God's people. With the priest we make the Sign of the Cross. The priest reminds us that Jesus is present among us.

The priest invites us to remember that we need God's forgiveness. We think about the times that we might have sinned. We tell God that we are sorry and ask for forgiveness.

On most Sundays of the year, we sing or say the "Gloria." We praise and bless God for his great love and care. This hymn of praise begins with: "Glory to God in the highest."

Think about your parish's celebration of the Mass last week. With a partner talk about what happened in the Introductory Rites.

We listen to God's Word.

The Liturgy of the Word is the part of the Mass when we listen and respond to God's Word.

On Sundays and other special days, there are three readings from Scripture. The first reading is usually from the Old Testament. After this reading we sing or say a psalm from the Old Testament. Then the second reading is from the New Testament. The readers end the first and second readings with: "The word of the Lord." We respond: "Thanks be to God."

The third reading is from one of the four Gospels: Matthew, Mark, Luke, or John. The Gospel is very special. We hear about the life and teachings of Jesus.

Before the Gospel we show we are ready to hear the Good News of Jesus Christ. We do this by standing and singing the Alleluia. The deacon or priest then proclaims the Gospel. To proclaim the Gospel means to announce the Good News with praise and glory. At the end of the Gospel the deacon or priest says: "The Gospel of the Lord."

We respond: "Praise to you, Lord Jesus Christ."

After the Gospel, the priest or deacon gives the homily. The homily helps us to understand what the three readings mean in our lives. Then we all stand and state our belief in God by saying the Creed.

In the *Prayer of the Faithful*, we pray for our Church and our world. We ask God to help our leaders, our family and friends, all those who are sick and in need, and all those who have died.

Who would you like to pray for at Mass this week? Write a prayer for them here.

_____

_____

_____

_____

_____

We receive Jesus Christ.

During the **Liturgy of the Eucharist** the bread and wine become the Body and Blood of Christ, which we receive in Holy Communion. The altar is prepared for this part of the Mass. Members of the assembly bring forward our gifts of bread and wine and our gifts for the Church and the poor.

The priest then asks God to bless and accept the gifts we will offer. We also offer our whole lives to God. Now the *Eucharistic Prayer* begins. It is the great prayer of praise and thanksgiving. The priest prays this prayer in our name to the Father through Jesus Christ. Through this prayer we are united with Christ.

The priest recalls all that God has done for us. We sing a song that begins: "Holy, holy, holy Lord."

The priest then says and does what Jesus said and did at the Last Supper. Through these words and actions of the priest, by the power of the Holy Spirit, the bread and wine become the Body and Blood of Christ. This part of the Eucharistic Prayer is called the *Consecration*. Jesus is truly present in the Eucharist. This is called the *Real Presence*.

At the end of the Eucharistic Prayer, we say or sing "Amen." Together we are saying "Yes, we believe."

Next we pray together the Lord's Prayer, the Our Father. We offer one another a sign of peace. The priest then breaks the Bread while the "Lamb of God" prayer is sung.

Then we all come forward to receive Holy Communion. We sing as we go to receive to show our unity with one another. After communion we all sit in silence.

In groups talk about ways we can show that we are united to Christ and one another.

We go out to love and serve the Lord.

As the Mass ends we are encouraged to share the Good News of Jesus with others. The last part of the Mass is the Concluding Rites. The **Concluding Rites** remind us to continue praising and serving God each day.

The priest says a final prayer thanking God for the Eucharist we have celebrated. He blesses us, and we make the Sign of the Cross. Then the priest or deacon, in Jesus' name, sends us out into the world. He may say, "Go in peace." We answer, "Thanks be to God."

We leave the church singing. With the help of the Holy Spirit, we try to help people who are in need. We do what we can to make our world a more loving and peaceful place. We try to treat others as Jesus would.

As Catholics...

After Holy Communion, the remaining consecrated Bread, or Hosts, are put in a special place in the church called the *tabernacle*. The Eucharist in the tabernacle is known as the *Blessed Sacrament*. The Blessed Sacrament can be taken to people who are dying and to those who are sick.

Jesus Christ is truly present in the Blessed Sacrament. Catholics honor Jesus' Real Presence by praying before the Blessed Sacrament.

The next time you are in church, kneel and pray to Jesus in the Blessed Sacrament.

WE RESPOND

 How could we love and serve others in these situations? Write your ideas.

• A family member is really tired.

We could:

_____

• A classmate is being "picked on."

We could:

_____

Key Words

Liturgy of the Eucharist (p. 252)

Concluding Rites (p. 250)

Pray Learn Celebrate Share Choose Live

PROJECT

Show What *you* Know

Put the four parts of the Mass in order, 1 to 4.

Liturgy of the Word	Concluding Rites	Introductory Rites	Liturgy of the Eucharist
_____	_____	_____	_____

Saint Stories

Katharine Drexel came from a rich family. She decided to use her money to help others. She worked for the rights of Native Americans and African Americans. She started a religious community called the Sisters of the Blessed Sacrament. She believed that Jesus invites all people to join the Church, take part in the Mass, and receive the Eucharist. Find out more about Saint Katharine on *Lives of the Saints* at **www.webelieveweb.com**.

Pray Today

Pray this prayer to remind you to love and serve the Lord.

Dear Jesus,
you are the light of my life,
you are the joy of my day,
you are my strength that helps me
    to serve you.
Jesus, to love you is to serve you and others.
Amen.

DISCIPLE

Pray
Learn
Celebrate
Share
Choose
Live

☀Celebrate!

Match these words we hear during the Liturgy of the Word with our response.

We hear

"The word of the Lord." ●

"A reading from the holy Gospel according to . . ." ●

"The Gospel of the Lord." ●

"For those who are sick, we pray to the Lord." ●

Our response

● "Praise to you, Lord Jesus Christ."

● "Lord, hear our prayer."

● "Glory to you, O Lord."

● "Thanks be to God."

Reality Check

Using the letters of the word AMEN, describe what you believe as a third grade disciple. The first one is done for you.

All people are loved by God.

M _____

E _____

N _____

Take Home

Prepare for Mass by visiting *This Week's Liturgy* at www.webelieveweb.com to see the readings for this Sunday's Mass. Use the reflection and discussion questions to talk about these readings with your family.

CHAPTER TEST

Write T if the sentence is true. Write F if the sentence is false.

1. _____ The first part of the Mass is called the Introductory Rites.

2. _____ We learn about the life and teachings of Jesus in the Gospel.

3. _____ The Liturgy of the Eucharist gets us ready to listen to God's Word.

4. _____ The Concluding Rites remind us to continue to praise God and to serve God and his people each day.

Does this take place during:
A: Liturgy of the Word or B: Liturgy of the Eucharist?

5. _____ The Gospel is proclaimed.

6. _____ The bread and wine become the Body and Blood of Christ.

7. _____ We receive Holy Communion.

8. _____ We state our belief in God by praying the Creed.

Write sentences to answer the questions.

9. What is one thing that happens during the Introductory Rites?

_____

10. The Concluding Rites remind us to continue praising and serving God each day. How can we do this?

_____

Celebrating Penance and Reconciliation

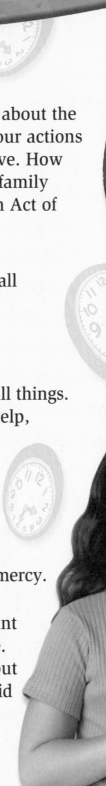

18

WE GATHER

✝ **Leader:** Sit quietly. Think about the last few days. Sometimes our actions and words do not show love. How have you acted with your family and friends? Let us pray an Act of Contrition together.

All: My God,
I am sorry for my sins with all
  my heart.
In choosing to do wrong
and failing to do good,
I have sinned against you
whom I should love above all things.
I firmly intend, with your help,
to do penance,
to sin no more,
and to avoid whatever
  leads me to sin.
Our Savior Jesus Christ
suffered and died for us.
In his name, my God, have mercy.

☀ Think about an important choice you had to make. What did you think about before choosing? How did you know whether you made the right choice?

155

WE BELIEVE
We make the choice to love God.

God wants us to love him, ourselves, and others. This is God's law. When we live by the Ten Commandments and follow Jesus' example we obey God's law.

However, there are times we do not live the way Jesus wants us to live. We freely choose to do what we know is wrong. We commit a sin. Sin is a thought, word, or action that is against God's law. Sin is always a choice. That is why mistakes and accidents are not sins.

Some sins are very serious. These serious sins are mortal sins. A *mortal sin* is:

- very seriously wrong
- known to be wrong
- freely chosen.

People who commit mortal sin turn away completely from God's love. They choose to break their friendship with God. They lose the gift of grace, their share in God's life and love.

Not all sins are mortal sins. Sins that are less serious are *venial sins*. People who commit venial sins hurt their friendship with God. Yet they still share in God's life and love.

 Write one way you can show that you have chosen to love God today.

_____

_____

God is our forgiving Father.

Jesus told this story to help us to understand God's love and forgiveness.

📖 Luke 15:11–32

sin (p. 253)

A rich man had two sons. One son wanted his share of the father's money. He wanted to leave home and have some fun. His father was sad, but he let his son have the money.

The son went away and began to spend his money. He used his money on all kinds of things. Soon all his money was gone.

The son found himself poor, dirty, hungry, and without friends. He thought about his father and his home. He decided to go home and tell his father that he was sorry.

When the father saw his son, he was so happy. The father rushed out and hugged him. The son said, "Father, I have sinned against heaven and against you; I no longer deserve to be called your son." (Luke 15:21)

But the father wanted everyone to know his son had come home. The father shouted to his servants, "Let us celebrate with a feast." (Luke 15:23)

Jesus told this story to show that God is our loving Father. He is always ready to forgive us when we are sorry.

We receive God's forgiveness through the Church. Our relationship with God and the Church is made strong through the Sacrament of Penance and Reconciliation, which we can call the Sacrament of Penance.

🧒 Talk about times people forgive each other.

The Sacrament of Penance has several parts.

Examining our conscience is the first step in preparing for the Sacrament of Penance. Our **conscience** is God's gift that helps us know right from wrong.

When we examine our conscience, we ask ourselves whether or not we have loved God, others, and ourselves. We think about the things we have done and whether they were right or wrong. This examination of conscience helps us to know and to be sorry for our sins.

Contrition, confession, penance, and absolution are always part of the Sacrament of Penance.

Contrition is being sorry for our sins and firmly intending not to sin again. *Confession* is telling our sins to the priest. The priest may talk to us about the way we can love God and others.

A *penance* is a prayer or action that shows we are sorry for our sins. Accepting the penance shows that we are willing to change the way that we live. *Absolution* is God's forgiveness of our sins through the actions and words of the priest. The priest extends his hand and forgives us. He ends by saying,

"Through the ministry of the Church may God give you pardon and peace, and I absolve you from your sins in the name of the Father, and of the Son, † and of the Holy Spirit."

Write one reason why the Church celebrates the Sacrament of Penance.

•contrition•

•confession•

Key Word

conscience (p. 250)

As Catholics...

Many parishes have a separate space for celebrating the Sacrament of Penance. This is a special place where you meet the priest for individual confession and absolution. You can choose how you want to talk with the priest. You can sit and talk to him face-to-face or kneel behind a screen.

In your parish, where do you celebrate the Sacrament of Penance?

The Church celebrates the Sacrament of Penance.

The Sacrament of Penance is a celebration of God's love and forgiveness. Here are two ways the Church celebrates the Sacrament of Penance.

Celebrating with the Community

We sing an opening hymn and the priest greets us and prays an opening prayer.

We listen to a reading from the Bible and a homily.

We examine our conscience and pray an Act of Contrition. We pray the Our Father.

I meet individually with the priest and confess my sins. The priest talks to me about loving God and others. He gives me a penance.

The priest extends his hand and gives me absolution.

After everyone has met with the priest, we join together to conclude the celebration. The priest blesses us, and we go in the peace and joy of Christ.

Celebrating Individually

The priest greets me. I make the Sign of the Cross.

The priest or I may read something from the Bible.

I meet individually with the priest and confess my sins. The priest talks to me about loving God and others. He gives me a penance.

I pray an Act of Contrition.

The priest extends his hand and gives me absolution.

Together the priest and I give thanks to God for his forgiveness.

WE RESPOND

How can you thank God for his forgiveness after celebrating the Sacrament of Penance?

absolution

Show What you Know

Find the **Key Words** hidden in the picture. Use them to answer the clues.

_____ is a thought, word, or action that is against God's law.

_____ is God's gift that helps us know right from wrong.

Now, color the picture.

Reality Check

How do you show someone forgiveness?

❏ say "I forgive you."

❏ plan to do something together

❏ shake hands

❏ other _____

_____

_____

Celebrate!

The Sacrament of Penance has four parts. Circle the parts you can explain to a classmate.

- contrition
- confession
- penance
- absolution

Now, pass it on!

DISCIPLE

Pray
Learn
Celebrate
Share
Choose
Live

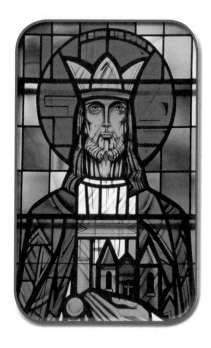

Saint Stories

King Edward ruled England from 1042 until his death in 1066. He was known for his generosity, holiness, and kindness as a ruler. In his time, the title of Confessor was given to saints who remained faithful to the Church, and were known for their knowledge, faith, and good works. So he is called Saint Edward the Confessor. His feast day is October 13th.

↳ **DISCIPLE CHALLENGE** Circle the title given to Saint Edward for his faithfulness to the Church.

Make it Happen

In 1981, Pope John Paul II was nearly killed when he was shot by Mehmet Ali Agca. The pope was hurt badly, but he got well. The pope visited Agca in prison and told him that he forgave him. The pope's willingness to forgive is an example to all of us. We are called to forgive those who hurt us.

↳ **DISCIPLE CHALLENGE** How will you answer the call to forgive those who hurt you?

_____

_____

_____

_____

Take Home

Watch a television series with your family. Then talk together about these questions.

• What choices did the characters in the series have to make?

• How were these good choices?

• How could they have made better choices?

CHAPTER TEST

Name each part of the Sacrament of Penance.

1. A prayer or action that shows we are sorry for our sins _____

2. Telling our sins to the priest _____

3. Being sorry for our sins and intending not to sin again _____

4. God's forgiveness of our sins through the words and
   actions of the priest _____

Fill in the circle beside the correct answer.

5. God is _____ willing to forgive us when we are truly sorry.
   ○ never   ○ sometimes   ○ always

6. Our _____ is God's gift that helps us to know right from wrong.
   ○ conscience   ○ contrition   ○ confession

7. Through Penance our relationship with God and the Church is _____.
   ○ weakened   ○ made strong   ○ broken

8. When we pray an Act of _____, we tell God we are sorry for our sins.
   ○ Contrition   ○ Confession   ○ Conscience

Write sentences to answer the questions.

9. What is sin?

   _____

10. What do we do when we examine our conscience?

   _____

WE GATHER

✝ **Leader:** Jesus asked people to believe in him. He healed those who had faith in him. Let us rejoice and sing this song:

🎵 **Walking Up to Jesus**

So many people in the house with
  Jesus,
People, people, people come to see
  him!

Jesus looked, and said to the man
  who could not walk:
"Get up now. You are healed.
  You can walk!"
And all at once the man jumped up
  and everyone said, "OH!"

For he was walking in the house
  with Jesus,
Walking, walking,
  walking up to Jesus!

☀ Think of a time when you felt hurt or sick. Who helped you? How did you feel after they helped you?

Jesus cared for and healed the sick.

Jesus cared for all people. When those who were sick, hungry, poor, or in need reached out to him, Jesus comforted them. Sometimes he cured them of their illnesses. He gave them a reason to hope in God's love and care.

 Mark 10:46–52

Jesus was leaving a town with his disciples and a large crowd. A blind man named Bartimaeus was sitting by the side of the road. He called out to Jesus to have pity on him. People in the crowd told Bartimaeus to be quiet. But he kept calling out to Jesus anyway.

"Jesus stopped and said, 'Call him.' So they called the blind man, saying to him, 'Take courage; get up, he is calling you.' He threw aside his cloak, sprang up, and came to Jesus. Jesus said to him in reply, 'What do you want me to do for you?'

The blind man replied to him, 'Master, I want to see.' Jesus told him, 'Go your way; your faith has saved you.' Immediately he received his sight and followed him on the way." (Mark 10:49–52)

Act out this Gospel story.

Jesus listened to people who needed his help. Jesus often visited the homes of people who were sick. Wherever he went people asked Jesus to help and to heal them.

Jesus wants us to have his comfort and peace, too. No matter what our needs are Jesus gives us hope and the joy of his love.

The Church heals us in Jesus' name.

Today the Church carries on Jesus' healing work. One of the most important ways is in the Sacrament of the Anointing of the Sick. Through the sacrament, those who are sick receive God's grace and comfort. The Holy Spirit helps them to trust in God's love. The Holy Spirit helps them to remember that God is always with them.

Any Catholic who is seriously ill may receive the Anointing of the Sick. Those in danger of death, for example, or those about to have a major operation are encouraged to celebrate this sacrament.

The oil of the sick is holy oil that has been blessed by the bishop for use in the Anointing of the Sick. A priest anoints the forehead of each sick person with this oil, saying:

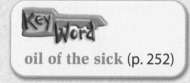

Key Word

oil of the sick (p. 252)

"Through this holy anointing may the Lord in his love and mercy help you with the grace of the Holy Spirit."

The priest also anoints the hands of each sick person, saying:
"May the Lord who frees you from sin save you and raise you up."

Family and parish members join with those who are elderly or sick in celebrating this sacrament. The Anointing of the Sick is a sacrament for the whole Church. We all pray that God will heal the sick, and we remember our own call to follow Jesus by loving and caring for people who are sick.

With a partner talk about some times people may need Jesus' comfort and hope. Write one way we can help them.

We believe in eternal life with God.

Sometimes people may be so sick that they do not get better. We pray that they will not feel lonely and sad. We pray that they will trust in Jesus' promise to be with them always. Jesus will be with them at their death as he was during their life.

Death is not easy for us to understand or to accept. As Christians we do not see death as the end of life. We believe that our life continues after death, in a different way. We call this eternal life. **Eternal life** is living forever with God in the happiness of Heaven.

When people choose to love and serve God and others, they will live with God forever. Heaven is life with God forever.

Some people choose not to love and serve God. Some people choose to break their friendship with God completely. Because of this choice, they separate themselves from God forever. Hell is being separated from God forever.

God does not want anyone to be separated from him. Yet many people who die in God's friendship may not be ready to enter the happiness of Heaven. These people enter into Purgatory, which prepares them for Heaven. Our prayers and good works can help these people so they may one day be with God in Heaven.

🏃 Name some ways that the choices we make show God that we are his friends.

As Catholics...

The Church encourages us to remember and pray for those who have died. One way we can do this is by having a Mass offered in their memory. A Mass card is given to the family of the person who has died. This Mass card lets the family know that a priest will be offering a Mass for their loved one. The family is given comfort knowing that the person who has died is being remembered.

Next time you are at Mass, remember to offer a prayer for a family member, relative, or friend who has died.

The Church celebrates eternal life with God.

No one can take away the sadness that we feel when someone we love dies. Even though we are sad, Catholics trust that this person will enjoy eternal life.

At a special Mass we thank God for the life of the person who has died. This Mass is called a **funeral Mass**. We gather as the Church with the family and friends of the person who has died. We pray that this person will share life with God forever.

The funeral Mass gives us hope. We are reminded that:

- at Baptism we were joined to Christ
- Jesus died and rose from the dead to bring us new life
- death can be the beginning of eternal life.

At the funeral Mass we pray that the person who has died will be joined to Christ in Heaven. We celebrate our belief that everyone who has died in Christ will live with him forever. We give comfort to the person's family and friends by spending time and praying with them.

WE RESPOND

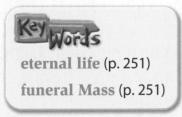 Design a card for someone who might need comfort and hope.

Key Words

eternal life (p. 251)
funeral Mass (p. 251)

167

PROJECT

Show What you Know

Answer the following questions by writing the letter that comes BEFORE the given letter in the alphabet. Your answers are the Key Words.

A	B	C	D	E	F	G	H	I	J	K	L	M	N	O	P	Q	R	S	T	U	V	W	X	Y	Z

1. What is blessed by the bishop for use in the Anointing of the Sick?

___ ___ ___   ___ ___   ___ ___ ___   ___ ___ ___ ___
 P   J   M   P   G   U   I   F   T   J   D   L

2. What is living forever with God in the happiness of Heaven?

___ ___ ___ ___ ___ ___ ___   ___ ___ ___ ___
 F   U   F   S   O   B   M   M   J   G   F

3. What is the special Mass to thank God for the life of a person who died?

___ ___ ___ ___ ___ ___ ___   ___ ___ ___ ___
 G   V   O   F   S   B   M   N   B   T   T

Fast Facts The Catholic Health Association of the United States (CHA) was established in 1915. They continue Jesus' mission of love and healing. Their health care facilities welcome and care for people of all ages, races, and religious beliefs.

DISCIPLE

Pray
Learn
Celebrate
Share
Choose
Live

Saint Stories

Saint Raphael the Archangel has great healing power. In the Bible, we read that Raphael was sent by God to help a man named Tobit. The Church teaches that Saint Raphael is the healing angel. The name *Raphael* means, "God has healed!"

↳ **DISCIPLE CHALLENGE** Find out when we celebrate the Feast of Saint Raphael.

_____

Make it Happen

Following the example of Jesus, Catholics show respect for all people. Parishes provide help to the sick, the elderly, and the dying. Priests, deacons, and extraordinary ministers of Holy Communion visit these people. They read from the Bible, pray together, and offer Holy Communion. You can also help by praying, sending cards, or by visiting with your family. As a class, plan one way to help those who are sick in your parish.

_____

_____

_____

Take Home

Invite your family to remember someone who has died. Make time as a family to share stories about that person. Together as a family, pray for that person.

169

CHAPTER TEST

Complete the sentences.

1. In the Sacrament of the Anointing of the Sick, the priest anoints a sick person with the _____.

2. _____ is living forever with God in the happiness of Heaven.

3. A _____ is a special Mass at which we thank God for the life of a person who has died.

Write T if the sentence is true. Write F if the sentence is false.

4. _____ People who will have a major operation are discouraged from celebrating the Sacrament of the Anointing of the Sick.

5. _____ The priest anoints the sick person's forehead and hands.

6. _____ In the Anointing of the Sick, the Church heals in Jesus' name.

7. _____ Family and friends are discouraged from taking part in the celebration of the Sacrament of the Anointing of the Sick.

8. _____ Purgatory is being separated from God forever.

Answer the following.

9. Write one way Jesus helped people who were sick.

_____

_____

10. Write one thing we are reminded of during a funeral Mass.

_____

"Come to me heedfully,
listen, that you may have life."

Isaiah 55:3

SEASONAL
CHAPTER 20

This chapter offers preparation for
the season of Lent.

> **The season of Lent is a time of preparation for Easter.**

WE GATHER

Have you had to take the time to get ready for a special event like a family get-together?

How did you prepare?

What did you do?

WE BELIEVE

Lent is our time of preparation for Easter. All during Lent, we remember three very important things:

- We belong to God through Baptism.
- We live now by grace, the life of God within us.
- We will live forever with God because Jesus died and rose to bring us God's life.

The season of Lent lasts forty days. It begins on Ash Wednesday. On this day we are marked with blessed ashes. The ashes are used to make a cross on our foreheads. The ashes are a sign that we are sorry for our sins and that we look forward to life with God forever.

Ashes

We rise again from ashes,
from the good we've failed to do.
We rise again from ashes,
to create ourselves anew.
If all our world is ashes,
then must our lives be true,
an offering of ashes,
an offering to you.

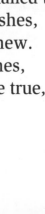

Lent is a special time for the Church. It is a special time to renew our Baptism. We remember the waters of Baptism that cleansed us from sin and brought us new life. We recall that in Baptism we were joined to Jesus and first received a share in God's life, grace. This is the grace we also receive in the Eucharist and the other sacraments.

Celebrating the Sacraments of Penance and the Eucharist is an important part of the season of Lent. The sacraments bring us into the wonder of Christ's Death and Resurrection. We are strengthened by God's love and forgiveness. We are nourished by the Body and Blood of Christ.

Lent is a time to grow in faith. We think and pray about the life we have because Jesus died and rose for us. We think about what we believe as Christians. We pray with those who will celebrate the Sacraments of Christian Initiation at the Easter Vigil.

During Lent we make a special effort to follow Jesus. We do this through prayer, penance, and acts of love and mercy. Doing these things during Lent helps us to renew our Baptism and gets us ready for the great Three Days.

Caring For Our Community

Catholic Diocese of Gary
and
Northwest Indiana Habitat for Humanity

OPERATION RICE BOWL

Catholic Relief Services

WE RESPOND

Talk together with your class about what you can do to grow in faith and love during Lent. Write some of the ideas suggested.

_____

_____

_____

_____

Look back at what you have written. Put a check beside the things you would like to do.

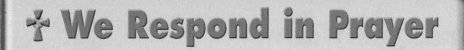

✝ We Respond in Prayer

Leader: O merciful God, you loved us so much you sent your Son to bring us life. Help us to believe in and follow him.

All: We believe!

Reader: A reading from the Gospel of John

"For God so loved the world that he gave his only Son, so that everyone who believes in him might not perish but have eternal life. For God did not send his Son into the world to condemn the world, but that the world might be saved through him." (John 3:16–17)

The Gospel of the Lord.

All: Praise to you, Lord Jesus Christ.

🎵 **Ashes**

Thanks be to the Father,
who made us like himself.
Thanks be to his Son,
who saved us by his death.
Thanks be to the Spirit
who creates the world anew
From an offering of ashes,
an offering to you.

PROJECT DISCIPLE

Pray Learn Celebrate Share Choose Live

Show What *you* Know

What do you know about Lent?

- How many days are in Lent? _____
- What are we marked with as we begin Lent?

  _____

- What is the Church's color for the season of

  Lent? _____

- What are we preparing for during Lent? _____
- What sacraments are important parts of the season of Lent?

  _____

What's *the* Word?

Jesus said to them,
"Thus it is written that the Messiah would suffer and rise from the dead on the third day." (Luke 24:46)

This is what we remember during Lent—that Jesus suffered, died, and rose for us.

Now, pass it on!

Take Home

Look at the Stations of the Cross on page 244. Ask a family member to help you find out when your parish community joins together to pray the stations during Lent. Mark the dates on your family calendar, and plan for everyone to attend.

"Most blessed of all nights,
chosen by God
to see Christ rising from the dead!"

Exsultet, Easter Vigil

SEASONAL

CHAPTER 21

This chapter includes the three days from Holy Thursday evening until Easter Sunday.

The Three Days celebrate that Jesus passed from death to new life.

WE GATHER

When have you celebrated a long weekend or holiday with your family?

What did you do or say that made it a special time to be with your family?

WE BELIEVE

The Three Days are the Church's greatest celebration. They are like a bridge. The Three Days take us from the season of Lent to the season of Easter.

Adoration before the Blessed Sacrament, Holy Thursday night

During the Three Days, we gather with our parish. We celebrate at night and during the day. The Three Days are counted from evening to evening. The first day starts on the evening of Holy Thursday. We remember what happened at the Last Supper. We celebrate that Jesus gave himself to us in the Eucharist. We remember the ways Jesus served others. We have a special collection for those who are in need.

On Good Friday, we remember the suffering and Death of Jesus on the cross. In church, the altar is completely bare. We listen to the Bible readings that tell us about Jesus' Death. We give special honor to the cross, and we praise God for the life that comes from Jesus' Death. We pray for the whole world. Then we wait and pray.

Reading of the Passion, Good Friday

Easter candle lit by Easter fire, Easter Vigil

On Holy Saturday, we think about all that happened to Jesus. We pray that we might be joined to Jesus. We gather again as a community at night for the Easter Vigil. A fire is burning bright. The Easter candle is lit and we sing "Christ our light!"

We listen to many different stories from the Bible. We remember all the great things God has done for us. We sing with joy to celebrate that Jesus rose from the dead.

New members of the Church receive the new life of Christ in Baptism, Confirmation, and the Eucharist. We rejoice with them. This is the most important and the most beautiful night of the year! Holy Saturday turns into Easter Sunday.

On Easter Sunday, we listen to the story of Jesus' Resurrection. We receive the Body and Blood of the risen Jesus in Holy Communion. We are given new strength and joy to live his risen new life. Alleluia!

WE RESPOND

In the space below, draw or write something that will tell others about the Three Days.

Paschal candle and baptismal font, Easter Sunday

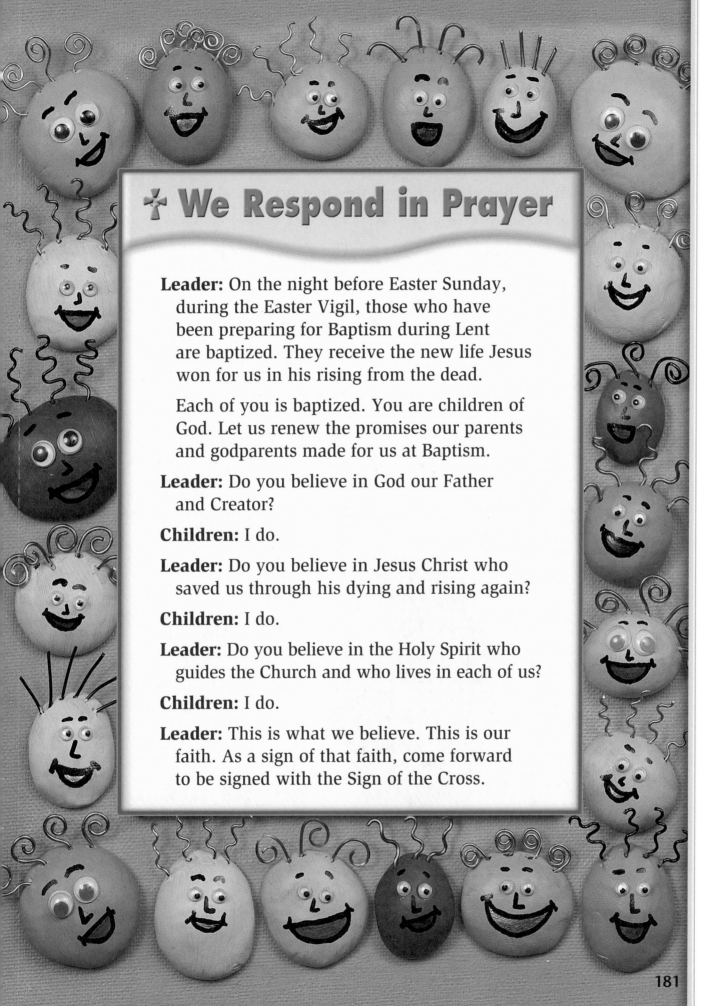

✝ We Respond in Prayer

Leader: On the night before Easter Sunday, during the Easter Vigil, those who have been preparing for Baptism during Lent are baptized. They receive the new life Jesus won for us in his rising from the dead.

Each of you is baptized. You are children of God. Let us renew the promises our parents and godparents made for us at Baptism.

Leader: Do you believe in God our Father and Creator?

Children: I do.

Leader: Do you believe in Jesus Christ who saved us through his dying and rising again?

Children: I do.

Leader: Do you believe in the Holy Spirit who guides the Church and who lives in each of us?

Children: I do.

Leader: This is what we believe. This is our faith. As a sign of that faith, come forward to be signed with the Sign of the Cross.

Pray
Learn
Celebrate
Share
Choose
Live

Grade 3 The Three Days

PROJECT DISCIPLE

Show What *you* Know

Draw lines to match each day to a way to celebrate it.

Holy Thursday ●

Good Friday ●

Holy Saturday ●

Easter Sunday ●

● The Easter candle is lit and we sing "Christ our light!"

● We celebrate that Jesus gave himself to us in the Eucharist.

● We listen to the story of Jesus' Resurrection.

● We give special honor to the cross, and we praise God for the life that comes from Jesus' Death.

Celebrate!

At the Easter Vigil Mass, new members of the Church receive the new life of Christ in the Sacraments of Baptism, Confirmation, and the Eucharist.

Write what you would tell a newly baptized person about being a Catholic.

_____

_____

Take Home

Pray this prayer with your family during the Three Days also known as the Triduum:

Jesus, we know you are with us in the Eucharist.

Jesus, we know your great love for us by your Death on the cross.

Jesus, we know you guide us always by the light of your Resurrection. Amen.

Use the words in the box to complete the sentences.

1. Baptism, Confirmation, and the Eucharist are Sacraments
   of Christian _____.

2. The _____ is the celebration of the Eucharist.

3. God's forgiveness of our sins through the words and
   actions of the priest is _____.

4. The Mass is a meal and a _____.

5. Our _____ is God's gift that helps us to
   know right from wrong.

> sacrifice
>
> healing
>
> Initiation
>
> conscience
>
> Mass
>
> absolution

Write T if the sentence is true. Write F if the sentence is false.

6. _____ We commit a sin when we know that a thought, word or
   action is wrong, but we do it anyway.

7. _____ Anointing of the Sick and Penance and Reconciliation
   are the Sacraments of Service to others.

8. _____ During the Sacrament of Penance, we pray an Act of Contrition.

9. _____ The most important prayer of the Mass is "Lord, have mercy."

10. _____ The Last Supper is the meal Jesus shared with his disciples
    on the night before he died.

continued on next page

continued on next page

The pictures show the two main parts of the Mass. Label the part shown in each picture. Then write a short description of this part.

11–12.

_____

_____

_____

_____

_____

13–14.

_____

_____

_____

_____

_____

15. At the end of Mass, the priest sends us out to love and serve God. Write a few ways that you can do this.

_____

_____

We Are Called to Discipleship

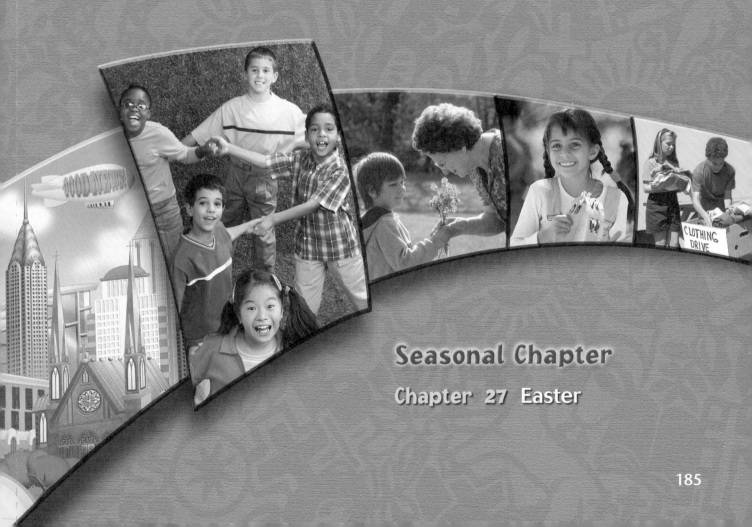

Seasonal Chapter

Pray
Learn
Celebrate
Share
Choose
Live

PROJECT DISCIPLE
DEAR FAMILY

In Unit 4 your child will grow as a disciple of Jesus by:

- living out the Good News of Jesus by working for peace and justice as Jesus did

- learning about our Jewish roots, and Jesus' prayer that all Christians will be united

- appreciating the one faith that all Catholics share, and the different ways they celebrate their faith

- remembering that we all belong to the Communion of Saints, and honoring Mary and all the saints

- recognizing Jesus' miracles as signs of the Kingdom of God, and learning about ways of spreading the Kingdom of God.

Make it Happen

Your child will understand more fully that one way we honor Mary is to pray the Rosary. Read page 214. As a family, this month make the decision to pray a decade of the Rosary each week. You might also decorate your family prayer space with pictures of Mary.

Saint Stories

The Communion of Saints unites us with all the members of the Church who are living and with those who have died and are in Heaven or Purgatory. Talk about your relatives and friends who have died. How were they examples of holiness? What good work might you do in memory of them?

Reality Check

"Becoming a disciple of Jesus means accepting the invitation to belong to *God's family*, to live in conformity with His way of life."

(*Catechism of the Catholic Church*, 2233)

More to Explore

Search the stories of your family members' patron saints online. How did each saint help to spread the Good News of Jesus? Pray to these saints, asking for help to be faithful disciples of Jesus. Start at www.webelieveweb.com, *Lives of the Saints*.

Pray Today

Offer a prayer for all Christians, that we may be one, as Jesus prayed we would be. If you have relatives, friends or neighbors who belong to other Christian churches, invite them for a visit, or share a meal together.

Take Home

Be ready for:

Chapter 22: Working for peace and justice

Chapter 23: Showing respect for all people

Chapter 24: Identifying family customs

Chapter 25: Praying to Mary together

Chapter 26: Learning about God's Kingdom

We Continue the Work of Jesus

WE GATHER

✝ **Leader:** Imagine that you are with the Apostles. Jesus has just been crucified. You are praying together in a room.

(Pause)

All of a sudden, Jesus is standing in the room with you. He says,

Reader 1: "Peace be with you." (John 20:19)

Leader: Think about the way you feel seeing Jesus again.

(Pause)

Now Jesus looks at you and says,

Reader 2: "As the Father has sent me, so I send you." (John 20:21)

Leader: What do you think Jesus means? Where is he sending you?

(Pause)

Let us pray together:

All: Jesus, we are listening to the message you have for each of us. You are sending us out to share the Good News that you have saved us. Help us as we go out to share your love with others. Amen.

Tell about a time when you were given something important to do. How did doing this help you, your family, or your friends?

187

WE BELIEVE
Jesus brings God's life and love to all people.

Jesus, the Son of God, had very important work to do. His mission was to bring God's life and love to all people.

 Luke 4:16–19

Jesus began his work among the people after he was baptized by his cousin John. In the synagogue in Nazareth, Jesus read these words from the prophet Isaiah.

"The Spirit of the Lord is upon me,
   because he has anointed me
      to bring glad tidings to the poor.
He has sent me to proclaim liberty to captives
   and recovery of sight to the blind,
      to let the oppressed go free,
and to proclaim a year acceptable to
   the Lord." (Luke 4:18–19)

Jesus then went to many towns and villages telling people that God cared for and loved them. Jesus showed those who were poor or lonely that they were important. He healed people who were sick. He stood up for those who were treated unjustly. Jesus cared for the people's needs and taught his disciples to do the same.

Jesus offered others the peace and freedom that come from God's love and forgiveness. He shared God's love with them, and they believed.

Jesus asks his disciples to care for the needs of others. Name one way you can do this.

Jesus shares his mission with his disciples.

Jesus gave his Apostles a mission. Jesus asked the Apostles to go to all nations and teach people about him. The Apostles were to baptize all those who believed in him.

The Holy Spirit strengthened and guided the Apostles. The Apostles led the other disciples in doing the work of Jesus. This is the Good News they shared:

- God made all people in his image.

- God loves and cares for everyone.

- God so loved the world that he sent his only Son who showed us how to live and saved us from sin.

- Jesus taught us to love God above all else and to love our neighbors as ourselves.

- Jesus worked for justice and peace and he asks all of us to do the same.

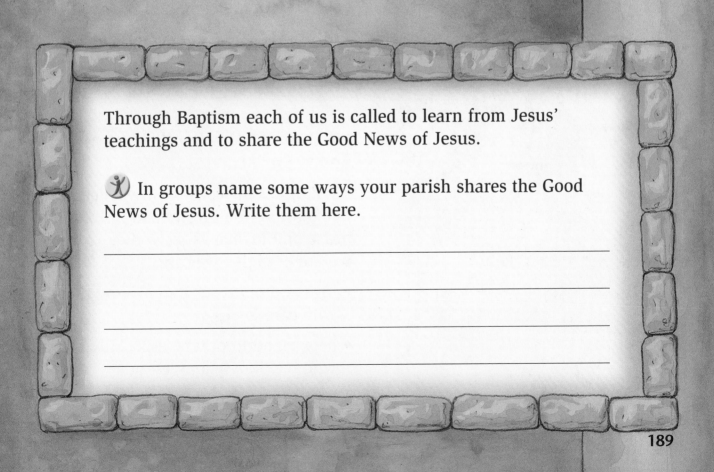

Through Baptism each of us is called to learn from Jesus' teachings and to share the Good News of Jesus.

In groups name some ways your parish shares the Good News of Jesus. Write them here.

_____

_____

_____

_____

The Church works for justice and peace.

Jesus taught that all people are created and loved by God. We are all made in God's image. So all people deserve to be treated fairly and with respect. Making sure this happens is one way the Church works for justice and peace in the world.

The pope and bishops teach us about the need to protect human life. In many ways they remind us to respect the rights of all people.

Our parishes serve those in need and work together to build better communities. In our families, schools, and neighborhoods, we live out Jesus' command to love others as he loves us.

The whole Church works for justice. We help to protect children, to care for the poor, and to welcome people who are new to our country.

With a partner come up with a slogan to remind your class about the need for justice and peace.

We live out the Good News of Jesus Christ.

As disciples of Jesus we are called to live out the Good News and to work for peace and justice as Jesus did. To show we are disciples we can:

- love and obey our parents and those who care for us

- be a friend to others, especially those who feel lonely and left out

- help those who are treated unfairly

- treat everyone fairly and with respect
- learn about and care for people who need our help in this country and in the world.

As disciples of Jesus we do not work alone. Together with other Church members, we can visit those who are sick or elderly. We can volunteer in soup kitchens or homeless shelters. We can help those who have disabilities. We can help those from other countries to find homes and jobs and to learn the language. We can write to the leaders of our state and country. We can ask our leaders for laws that protect children and those in need.

WE RESPOND

 Draw one way your family can bring Jesus' love to others.

As Catholics...

Both at home and in other countries, missionaries help to do the work of Jesus. They may be ordained priests and deacons, religious sisters and brothers, and single or married laypeople. Some missionaries serve as teachers, nurses, doctors, or social workers.

Some people spend their whole lives being missionaries. Others spend a month, a summer, or even a year or two doing missionary work.

Find out about some missionaries in your neighborhood.

PROJECT

Show What *you* Know

Unscramble the letters of the words. Then use the letters that match the numbers to complete the sentence.

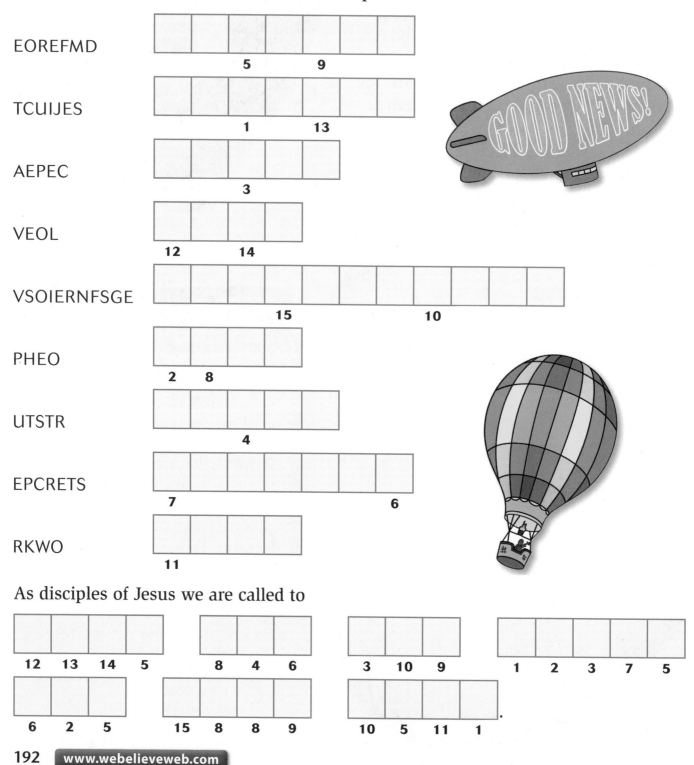

EOREFMD
☐ ☐ ☐ ☐ ☐ ☐ ☐
　　　　5　　　9

TCUIJES
☐ ☐ ☐ ☐ ☐ ☐ ☐
　　　1　　　13

AEPEC
☐ ☐ ☐ ☐ ☐
　　3

VEOL
☐ ☐ ☐ ☐
12　　14

VSOIERNFSGE
☐ ☐ ☐ ☐ ☐ ☐ ☐ ☐ ☐ ☐ ☐
　　　15　　　　10

PHEO
☐ ☐ ☐ ☐
2　8

UTSTR
☐ ☐ ☐ ☐ ☐
　　4

EPCRETS
☐ ☐ ☐ ☐ ☐ ☐ ☐
7　　　　　　6

RKWO
☐ ☐ ☐ ☐
11

GOOD NEWS!

As disciples of Jesus we are called to

☐ ☐ ☐ ☐　　☐ ☐ ☐　　☐ ☐ ☐　　☐ ☐ ☐ ☐ ☐
12 13 14 5　　8 4 6　　3 10 9　　1 2 3 7 5

☐ ☐ ☐　　☐ ☐ ☐ ☐　　☐ ☐ ☐ ☐ .
6 2 5　　15 8 8 9　　10 5 11 1

DISCIPLE

Pray
Learn
Celebrate
Share
Choose
Live

Pray Today

Jesus, you gave your disciples a mission. You asked them to share your work of bringing God's life and love to all people. You ask us to do the same. Help me to be a part of your mission. Amen.

What Would *you* do?

A family moves into your neighborhood. They have children close to your age. What would you do to show them that you are living out the Good News of Jesus Christ?

_____

_____

_____

Now, pass it on!

Reality Check

Check the ways you will live out the Good News of Jesus Christ. This week, I will:

❏ love and obey those who care for me

❏ be a friend to others, especially those who feel left out

❏ help those who are treated unfairly

❏ treat everyone fairly and with respect

❏ welcome a neighbor

❏ learn about people who need our help.

❏ other _____

Take Home

With your family, find out ways that your parish works for peace and justice. Decide on one way that your family can join in that work. Write it here and work together to do it.

_____

_____

193

Write T if the sentence is true. Write F if the sentence is false.

1. _____ We show we are disciples only when we participate at Mass.

2. _____ Jesus asks his disciples to continue his work.

3. _____ Only the pope and bishops share the Good News of Jesus.

4. _____ All people deserve to be treated fairly and with respect.

5. _____ As disciples of Jesus we only work alone.

Use the words in the box to complete the sentences.

6. Jesus' mission was to bring God's _____ and love to all people.

7. Jesus asked his _____ to go to all nations and teach people about him.

8. After Jesus returned to his Father in Heaven, the _____ strengthened and guided the Apostles.

> Apostles
>
> Holy Spirit
>
> justice
>
> life

9. All members of the Church are called to work for _____ and peace in every way they can.

Answer the following.

10. Write one way we can show we are Jesus' disciples.

_____

_____

The Church Respects All People

WE GATHER

✞ **Leader:** Let us sit quietly.
Thank God for his many blessings.
Now let us offer our prayers to him.

Reader: Let us pray
for all our brothers and sisters
who share our faith in Jesus Christ,
that God may gather and keep together
in one Church
all those who seek the truth
with sincerity.
We pray to the Lord.

All: Lord, hear our prayer.

Reader: Let us pray
for the Jewish People,
the first to hear the Word of God,
that they may continue to grow
in the love of his name
and in faithfulness to his covenant.
We pray to the Lord.

All: Lord, hear our prayer.

Leader: Almighty and eternal God,
enable those who do not
acknowledge Christ
to find the truth as they walk before you
in sincerity of heart.
We ask this through Christ our Lord.

All: Amen.

What interesting things have you learned
about people and places in other countries?
Talk about these things together.

WE BELIEVE

People around the world have different beliefs about God.

Christians are people of faith who believe in and follow Jesus Christ. Not everyone in the world believes in Jesus as Christians do. This does not mean that they are not people of faith. They believe in God and worship God in different ways. They live their faith at home, in school, and in their communities.

Jews are people of faith who keep God's law and follow the Ten Commandments. They worship God and celebrate many religious feasts.

Christians have a special connection to the Jewish people. Many Christian beliefs and practices come from the Jewish faith.

Muslims are people of faith who follow the teachings of Muhammad. They call God *Allah*. They pray and worship God in unique ways. Muslims have some of the same beliefs as Jews and Christians.

Many native tribes worship God by honoring and respecting his creation. They call God *the Great Spirit*.

There are many other people of faith. They, too, follow a set of beliefs and show their faith in different ways.

Look at the pictures on these pages. Are any of these faiths practiced in your town or city? Talk about ways you can show respect for people of all faiths.

Native American boy at powwow

Buddhist woman offering incense

Hindu festival

The Jewish faith is important to Christians.

Reading the Old Testament can help us to understand Jewish history and beliefs. This is important because they are part of our history, too. We learn from the Old Testament about God's covenant with Moses. A **covenant** is an agreement between God and his people.

In this covenant with Moses and the people, God promised to be their God. He would give his people a land all their own. The people promised to be God's people and to believe in him. They promised to worship only the one true God. They agreed to live by God's law and to follow the Ten Commandments.

God continued to love his people. He spoke to them through the prophets. The prophets reminded the people of their promises to God.

John the Baptist was one of these prophets. He told the prophets to ask God's forgiveness and to live by God's law. He prepared the people for the coming of the Messiah. The Messiah would be sent by God to bring mercy, peace, and justice.

Jesus was the Messiah. Some Jews believed this and followed Jesus. They became his disciples. After Jesus' Death and Resurrection, the number of Jesus' disciples grew. Those who followed Jesus and his teachings became known as Christians.

Muslims at prayer

Jewish Passover meal

covenant (p. 250)

In this scroll, write a prayer for God's blessings on our Jewish brothers and sisters.

_____

_____

_____

Christ calls his followers to be united.

At the Last Supper, Jesus prayed that his followers would always be one community. He prayed, "I pray not only for them, but also for those who will believe in me through their word, so that they may all be one . . ." (John 17:20–21)

Christians believe in and follow Jesus. Catholics are Christians. As Catholics we follow the teachings and example of Jesus Christ. We belong to the Catholic Church.

There are Orthodox Christians and Episcopal Christians. Other Christians may be Lutheran, Methodist, Presbyterian, and Baptist.

All Christians have some important things in common. All Christians are baptized and share some very important beliefs.

- God is Father, Son, and Holy Spirit.

- Jesus is both divine and human.

- Jesus died for our sins and rose again from the dead.

- The Bible was inspired by the Holy Spirit.

Today the Catholic Church is working with other Christians to bring together all baptized people. This work toward Christian unity is called **ecumenism**.

In groups list some things we can do to show that we are Christians. Share your ideas.

The Church works for Christian unity.

How can each one of us work for Christian unity? We first need to know our faith and be the best Catholics we can be. Other Christians can learn about the Catholic Church by who we are and what we do.

As Catholics...

Each year in January the Church celebrates a week of prayer for Christian Unity. We pray that all Christians may be one. Prayer services and discussion groups are held. Together Christians try to grow in love and understanding. As Catholics, every week at Mass we pray that all Christians will be one.

Find out how your parish works with other Christian churches in your neighborhood.

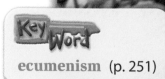
Key Word

ecumenism (p. 251)

We try to treat people the way Jesus did. We receive the sacraments. Receiving the sacraments is an important part of being Catholic. The sacraments strengthen our faith. The sacraments help us grow closer to God and to one another.

We also need to know our faith so we can share it with others. We cannot tell other people what it means to be a Catholic if we do not know. We read the Bible and ask God to help us to understand his Word. We learn the history of our Church. We also learn what the Church teaches about important topics. This helps us to follow the Church's teachings.

WE RESPOND

What is something you can do to show you are Christian?

Draw or write something that will encourage all Christians to work together for unity.

PROJECT

Pray
Learn
Celebrate
Share
Choose
Live

Show What *you* Know

Complete the crossword puzzle.

Down

1. _____ is work toward Christian unity.

2. _____ are people of faith who follow the teachings of Muhammad.

3. God spoke to his people through the _____.

8. Muslims call God _____.

Across

4. _____ are people of faith who keep God's law and follow the Ten Commandments.

5. A _____ is an agreement between God and his people.

6. _____ are people of faith who believe in and follow Jesus Christ.

7. John the Baptist prepared the people for the coming of the _____.

Pray Today

Jesus, you showed us how to treat others with love and respect. Amen.

DISCIPLE

Pray
Learn
Celebrate
Share
Choose
Live

What Would you do?

A close friend of yours is of another faith. You overhear a classmate making fun of your friend's faith. What would you do?

_____

_____

Fast Facts

Each year in January, Christians celebrate a week of prayer for Christian unity. It is a worldwide celebration. Christians are encouraged to pray together as a sign of unity. The week follows a theme that is based on the Bible. Some themes have been:

"Pray without ceasing." (1 Thessalonians 5:17)

"My peace I give to you." (John 14:27)

Reality Check

How can you live out the spirit of Christian unity?

❏ treat people the way Jesus did

❏ know the Catholic faith and share it

❏ learn the history of the Church

❏ learn about Church teaching

❏ pray for Christian unity

❏ other _____

Take Home

You might have family members, friends, or neighbors who practice a different faith than you do.

Talk about ways that your family can show respect for people of different faiths. Write some here.

_____

_____

CHAPTER TEST

Write T if the sentence is true. Write F if the sentence is false.

1. _____ Jews are people of faith who follow the Ten Commandments.

2. _____ Receiving the sacraments is not an important part of being Catholic.

3. _____ All Christians are baptized.

4. _____ As Catholics only some of us are called to work for Christian unity.

5. _____ All Christians believe that Jesus died for our sins and rose again from the dead.

Use the words in the box to complete the sentences.

6. A _____ is an agreement between God and his people.

7. John the Baptist was one of the _____ who reminded people about their promises to God.

8. The work toward Christian unity is called _____.

9. _____ are people of faith who follow the teachings of Muhammad.

ecumenism

Muslims

covenant

prophets

Answer the following.

10. Write one thing about the agreement between God and Moses and his people.

_____

_____

The Church Is Worldwide

Buena nueva

La bonne nouvelle

WE GATHER

✝ **Leader:** Let us gather quietly to listen to the Word of God.

Reader: A reading from the holy Gospel according to Luke

"He said to them, 'To the other towns also I must proclaim the good news of the kingdom of God, because for this purpose I have been sent.'" (Luke 4:43)

The Gospel of the Lord.

All: Praise to you, Lord Jesus Christ.

🎵 **We Are the Church**

Chorus
We are the Church,
   happy to be the children
   in God's family.

We are the Church,
   happy to be the children
   in God's family.

We are sharing the Good News.
We are sharing the Good News.
Ev'ryone old and young.
Ev'ryone weak and strong.

We are sharing the Good News,
   for (Chorus)

Il lieto messagio

Good News

☀ Do any of your family, friends, and neighbors come from another country? What do you know about that country?

WE BELIEVE

The Catholic Church is all over the world.

The Catholic Church is made up of people from all over the world. They have different customs. Customs are the way a group of people live, dress, and celebrate. The customs and history of each part of the world add beauty and wonder to the Church.

All around the world Catholics use their local customs to praise and worship God. In Africa drums and tribal dances are part of the celebration of the Mass. In Asia the Catholic Church celebrates with special traditions. For example, in Korea and in the Philippines, musical instruments and native costumes add to the celebration of the Mass.

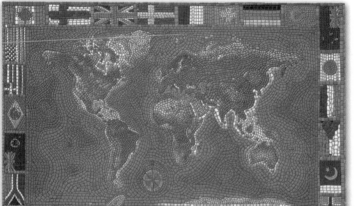

Many Catholics in the United States follow the customs of their native countries. For example, many Mexican Americans keep the custom of using luminarias. *Luminarias*, also called *faroles*, are paper sacks filled with sand and lighted candles. Before evening Masses luminarias are placed on paths leading to the church.

The Catholic Church is a wonderful mix of people with different languages, music, and customs. We are united by our faith in Jesus and our membership in the Church. We can all grow and learn from the customs of one another.

Immaculate Conception Church

If you could worship with Catholics in any part of the world, where would you choose to go? Why?

Catholics share the same faith.

Catholics in different parts of the world sometimes celebrate their Catholic faith in different ways. A **Rite** is a special way that Catholics celebrate and pray to God.

Most Catholics in the United States follow the Latin, or Roman, Rite. Other Catholics follow one of the Eastern Rites.

Catholics of the Eastern Rites and Latin Rite make up the whole Catholic Church. We are all joined together in three important ways.

- We all share the same beliefs. We state these beliefs in creeds such as the Apostles' Creed.

- We all celebrate the Seven Sacraments.

- With our bishops we are all united with the pope as one Church.

Catholics everywhere live as disciples of Jesus in their families, schools, and communities.

Think about Catholics in your neighborhood or city. Write one way they practice their faith.

_____

_____

As Catholics...

All Catholics are officially listed as members of the Catholic Church. In the parish where you were baptized, your name is written down in a special book called the *Baptismal Register*. Your name will always be there. As you celebrate other sacraments, they are also recorded in the Baptismal Register.

Find out the names of the parishes where your family members were baptized.

Key Word

Rite (p. 253)

Saint Michael's Russian Catholic Church

Catholics celebrate their faith in different ways.

Catholics celebrate and live out their faith in many ways. For example, all Catholics participate in the liturgy, the official public prayer of the Church.

However, the different Rites have different ways of celebrating. In the liturgy, the wording of some of the prayers is not always the same. The things the priest and people do are a little different, too.

The pictures on these pages show ways the Eastern Rites and the Latin Rite celebrate their Catholic faith. Talk about what the people in these pictures are doing. What is familiar to you? What questions might you have for the people in these pictures?

Receiving the Eucharist

Talk about ways your parish celebrates its faith. Then act one way out.

The altar at Curé of Ars Church

We are the light of the world.

As Catholics, we are united as one community. We are joined with Catholics all around the world. We pray and grow in holiness. No matter how we celebrate, we are all disciples of Jesus. We follow the beliefs and teachings handed down from the Apostles. Together we try to live, pray, and work as Jesus taught.

Jesus told his disciples, "You are the light of the world. Your light must shine before others, that they may see your good deeds and glorify your heavenly Father." (Matthew 5:14, 16)

Celebrating the Sacrament of Matrimony
at Saint Michael's Russian Catholic Church

Jesus calls each of us to be a light for all the world to see. When we share our gifts and talents for the good of others, we are a light in the world. When we follow Jesus' example, others can see the goodness of God. They can see the power of God's love in the world.

Receiving the Eucharist

WE RESPOND

Think about your gifts and talents. They could be things that you enjoy doing or things that you do well. How can you use your gifts and talents for the good of others? Draw one way you can shine for all the world to see.

PROJECT

Show What *you* Know

Color only the letter spaces with ▲. Then unscramble those letters to find the **Key Word** defined below.

A _____ is a special way that Catholics celebrate and pray to God.

● u	● g	▲ t	● c
▲ r	● x	● w	● f
● z	● j	● z	▲ e
● v	▲ i	● x	● o

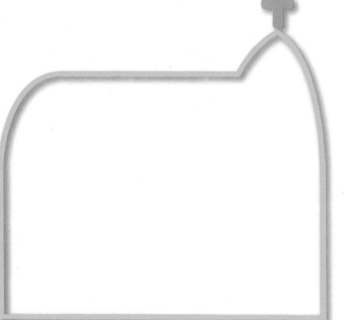

Picture This

The Catholic Church is a wonderful mix of people with different languages, music, and customs. Draw a picture to celebrate this fact.

↳ **DISCIPLE CHALLENGE** What is one custom that is celebrated in your parish? Add it to your picture.

Pray Today

Complete the prayer.

Heavenly Father, we are united by our belief in Jesus Christ, your Son. Help all members

of your Church to _____

_____ .

DISCIPLE

Pray
Learn
Celebrate
Share
Choose
Live

Fast Facts

The Catholic Church shows respect for the languages of its members. The Mass and the sacraments are celebrated in many languages, such as English, French, Spanish, Polish, Armenian, Greek, Latin, Ukrainian, Albanian, Romanian, Syrian, Coptic, and Ethiopian. The Mass and the sacraments are also celebrated in many Native American languages.

What's the Word?

Jesus said to the disciples,

"You are the light of the world. A city set on a mountain cannot be hidden. Nor do they light a lamp and then put it under a bushel basket; it is set on a lampstand, where it gives light to all in the house" (Matthew 5:14–15).

↳ **DISCIPLE CHALLENGE** What are some ways your parish can be a light for others to see?

_____

_____

_____

Take Home

What are some of your family's customs?

_____

_____

Talk about the reasons each one became a custom in your family. Which ones praise and worship God?

_____

_____

CHAPTER TEST

All Catholics are joined together in important ways. Check each sentence that states one of these ways.

1. _____ We celebrate Seven Sacraments.

2. _____ We dress the same and pray in the same language.

3. _____ We share the same beliefs and state them in creeds.

4. _____ With our bishops we are all united with the pope as one Church.

5. _____ Everyone celebrates and lives out his/her faith in exactly the same way.

Write T if the sentence is true. Write F if the sentence is false.

6. _____ A Rite is a special way Catholics celebrate and pray to God.

7. _____ Not all Catholics participate in the liturgy, the official public prayer of the Church.

8. _____ All members of the Church are called to follow Jesus' example, showing others the goodness of God.

Write sentences to answer the following.

9–10. You are a light in the world. Explain what this means and how you will share Jesus' light with others.

_____

_____

_____

We Are God's Holy People

Saint Peter

Saint Mary Magdalen

WE GATHER

✝ **Leader:** Let us sing a song to the saints.

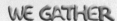 **Sing a Song to the Saints**

Chorus:
Sing a song to the saints,
the saints of God the most high.
Sing a song to the saints,
with names like yours and mine.

Saint Francis, pray for us.
Saint Cecilia, pray for us.
Saint Peter, pray for us.
Saint Mary Magdalen, pray for us.
Sing a song to the saints.

Saint George, pray for us.
Blessed Mary, pray for us.
Saint Thomas, pray for us.
Saint Anastasia, pray for us.
Sing a song to the saints.

Saint Benedict, pray for us.
Saint Margaret, pray for us.
Saint Joseph, pray for us.
Saint Elizabeth, pray for us.
Sing a song to the saints.

Saint Elizabeth of Hungary

☀ What are some ways we remember and honor special people who have lived before us?

Saint Francis

211

WE BELIEVE

We belong to the Communion of Saints.

God is holy. He shares his holiness with us when we are baptized. The word *saint* means "one who is holy." God calls all of us to be saints. **Saints** are followers of Christ who lived lives of holiness on earth and now share in eternal life with God in Heaven.

The saints are examples of holiness. We learn from them how to love God and care for others. Their lives show us how to be true disciples of Jesus.

The Church honors all the saints in Heaven in a special way on November 1. We call this day the Feast of All Saints. On this day we remember the holy people who have gone before us. We ask them to pray for us always.

Raphael (1483–1570),
The Madonna of the Chair

Edith Catlin Phelps (1875–1961),
Wayside Madonna

The union of the baptized members of the Church on earth with those who are in Heaven and in Purgatory is called the **Communion of Saints**. Through Baptism we are united to Christ and one another. We are united with all members of the Church who are alive on earth, and all who have died and are in Heaven or Purgatory.

Saints come from all over the world. Who are some saints you know about?

_____

_____

_____

Tell about them.

212

Mary is the greatest of all the saints.

Mary was blessed by God. She was free from Original Sin from the very first moment of her life. This belief is called the Immaculate Conception.

Mary was chosen by God and asked to be the Mother of his Son. Mary said, "May it be done to me according to your word" (Luke 1:38). Mary trusted God completely.

Mary loved and cared for Jesus. She listened to his teachings and saw the ways he treated others. She believed in him when others did not. She stayed at the cross as he was dying. She was with the disciples when the Holy Spirit first came to them.

When Mary's work on earth was done, God brought her body and soul to live forever with the risen Christ. This belief is called the Assumption.

Mary was Jesus' mother. She is the Mother of the Church, too. Jesus loved and honored his mother. The Church loves and honors Mary as well. When we remember Mary, we remember Jesus. We remember that God sent his Son to us.

Mary is an example for all of Jesus' disciples. Mary is the greatest of all the saints. We pray special prayers to honor Mary. The Hail Mary is one of these prayers. In the Hail Mary we praise Mary and ask her to pray for us.

 Talk about ways we can follow Mary's example. Then pray together the Hail Mary found on page 241.

Father John Giuliani,
Hopi Virgin and Child II

Key Words

saints (p. 253)

Communion of Saints (p. 250)

Immaculate Conception (p. 251)

Assumption (p. 250)

As Catholics...

A *canonized* saint is a person who has been officially named a saint by the Church. The life of this person has been examined by Church leaders. They have decided that the person has lived a life of faith and holiness.

When someone is canonized a saint, his or her name is entered into the worldwide list of saints recognized by the Catholic Church. Each canonized saint has a special feast day.

Is your parish named after a saint? What do you know about him or her?

The Church remembers and honors Mary.

Catholics all over the world honor Mary. We remember how God blessed her. We remember Mary when we celebrate Mass on her feast days.

Another way to honor Mary is by praying the Rosary. The Rosary combines many prayers. When we pray the Rosary, we recall special times in the lives of Mary and Jesus. The mysteries of the Rosary recall these special times. We remember a different mystery at the beginning of each decade, or set of ten small beads.

We use rosary beads like this one to pray the Rosary. Read these directions.

1. Start at the crucifix with the *Sign of the Cross.*

2. Then pray the *Apostles' Creed.*

3. Pray an *Our Father* at every large bead.

4. Pray a *Hail Mary* at every small bead.

5. Pray a *Glory be to the Father* after each set of small beads.

6. Pray the *Hail, Holy Queen* to end the Rosary.

With a partner discuss why the Rosary is a special prayer. Plan when you can pray the Rosary.

Joyful Mysteries

The Annunciation

The Visitation

The Birth of Jesus

The Presentation

The Finding of the Child Jesus in the Temple

Sorrowful Mysteries

The Agony in the Garden

The Scourging at the Pillar

The Crowning with Thorns

The Carrying of the Cross

The Crucifixion and Death of Jesus

Glorious Mysteries

The Resurrection

The Ascension

The Descent of the Holy Spirit upon the Apostles

The Assumption of Mary

The Coronation of Mary as Queen of Heaven

Mysteries of Light

Jesus' Baptism in the Jordan

The Miracle at the Wedding at Cana

Jesus Announces the Kingdom of God

The Transfiguration

The Institution of the Eucharist

We can also honor Mary by praying a litany. In a litany for Mary, we call on her by using some of her many titles. After the leader prays each title, we repeat a response.

God calls us to be saints.

The saints answered God's call to lead holy lives. Men, women, and children from every part of the world have become saints. Here are some examples:

Saint Louise de Marillac

- Saint Louise de Marillac was a wife and mother. After her husband died, she began the Daughters of Charity. They served the needs of people who were poor.

- Saint Charles Lwanga lived in Uganda, Africa. He was baptized as an adult. He helped many people in Africa, including those who served in the king's court, to become Christians.

- Saint Joan of Arc was a soldier in France. She tried her best to obey God's will.

- Saint Andrew Nam-Thuong was a mayor of a Vietnamese village. He taught others about the faith.

Saint Andrew Nam-Thuong

- Saint Dominic Savio was a boy who prayed to God everyday. Dominic saw God in the happenings of everyday life. He was always ready to help out a classmate.

God calls you to become a saint, too. How can you become a saint? You can know and live your faith every day. You can learn as much as possible about Jesus and the way he treated others. You can also find out more about the lives of the saints.

God helps each of us to be holy. We are strengthened by prayer. We receive grace from the sacraments. We also get support from our family and our parish. Together we can follow Jesus and grow in holiness.

WE RESPOND

With a partner list people who could be on a "Saints of Our Time" Web site. Give some reasons why they might be included.

_____

_____

_____

_____

_____

Show What *you* Know

Write a litany using the **Key Words**. Decorate the frame.

Assumption

Communion of Saints

Immaculate Conception

saints

_____, pray for us.

_____, _____.

_____, _____.

_____, _____.

Now, pass it on!

Make *it* Happen

God calls us to be saints. Some ways you can become a saint include:

- knowing and living your faith daily
- learning about Jesus and the way he treated others
- finding out more about the lives of the saints. (Visit *Lives of the Saints* at www.webelieveweb.com.)

↘ **DISCIPLE CHALLENGE** What is one more way to become a saint?

_____

DISCIPLE

Pray
Learn
Celebrate
Share
Choose
Live

Celebrate!

The Church sets aside a special day each year for remembering those who have died. This day is November 2, All Souls' Day. Take a moment this week to pray for those who have died.

Question Corner

Each title for Mary tells us something special about her. Survey three friends for their favorite titles for Mary. Write them here.

_____

_____

_____

from *The Nativity Story*, New Line Cinema, 2006

What's *the* Word?

"And Mary said:
'My soul proclaims the greatness of the Lord;
*   my spirit rejoices in God my savior.*
For he has looked upon his handmaid's lowliness;
*   behold, from now on will all ages call me*
*   blessed.'"* (Luke 1:46–48)

↳ DISCIPLE CHALLENGE

- Underline the phrase that tells who Mary rejoices in.

- Circle the word that describes Mary throughout the ages.

Take Home

Invite your family to pray the Hail Mary together each day this week. You might also pray the Rosary together.

CHAPTER TEST

Fill in the circle beside the correct answer.

1. The word _____ means "one who is holy."
   ○ saint   ○ rosary

2. The _____ is the belief that Mary was free from Original Sin from the very first moment of her life.
   ○ Assumption   ○ Immaculate Conception

3. The _____ is the belief that, when Mary's work on earth was done, God brought her body and soul to live forever with the risen Christ.
   ○ Assumption   ○ Immaculate Conception

4. God calls _____ to be saints.
   ○ all of us   ○ only some people

Write T if the sentence is true. Write F if the sentence is false.

5. _____ Only the saints in Heaven belong to the Communion of Saints.

6. _____ We repeat the *Hail, Holy Queen* on each small bead of the Rosary.

7. _____ When we pray the Joyful Mysteries of the Rosary, we recall Jesus' life as a young child.

8. _____ November 1 is the feast of Mary, Mother of God.

Answer the following.

9. Write one way Mary showed her love for Jesus.

_____

10. Write one way you can become a saint.

_____

WE GATHER

✝ **Leader:** The disciples of Jesus said to him, "Lord, teach us to pray." (Luke 11:1)

We, too, pray by following the teachings of Jesus. Let us pray the Lord's Prayer together.

Our Father, who art in heaven,
(head back, arms raised high)

hallowed be thy name;
(head down, arms crossed on chest)

thy kingdom come;
(right arm stretched out, palm up)

thy will be done on earth
(both arms pointing down to earth)

as it is in heaven.
(raise both arms to Heaven)

Give us this day our daily bread;
(cup hands in front)

and forgive us our trespasses
(hold cupped hands up high)

as we forgive those who trespass against us;
(take hands with those on either side)

and lead us not into temptation,
(hold right hand out, palm facing away)

but deliver us from evil.
(bring hand over heart)

Amen.
(bring both arms down to sides, head bowed, palms open)

Name a favorite story. What have you learned from this story?

WE BELIEVE

Jesus used parables to teach about the Kingdom of God.

Jesus wanted to teach the people about God's Kingdom. Many of them thought the Kingdom of God was about power and money. They thought it was like an earthly kingdom. But Jesus wanted everyone to know that the Kingdom of God is the power of God's love active in the world. To help them understand this, Jesus told the people parables, stories that use things from everyday life. A **parable** is a short story that has a message.

 Luke 13:18–19

Jesus told this parable: "What is the kingdom of God like? To what can I compare it? It is like a mustard seed that a person took and planted in the garden. When it was fully grown, it became a large bush and 'the birds of the sky dwelt in its branches.'" (Luke 13:18–19)

Jesus was telling his disciples that, although small, the Kingdom of God would grow as more people responded to God's love. When we believe in and follow Jesus Christ, we respond to God's love and his Kingdom grows.

 Name some signs of God's love active in our world today.

_____

_____

Jesus taught that the Kingdom of God will grow.

Jesus taught his disciples that the Kingdom of God is a kingdom of love. God's love was already active among them. Through Jesus' words and actions, the Kingdom had begun and would grow as more people followed him. Jesus told the following parable.

📖 Matthew 13:3–8; 18–23

Once there was a farmer who planted seeds in his field. Some seeds fell outside the field, on the path. The birds came and ate them. Other seeds fell on rocky ground. The rocky soil did not have enough water for the seeds to grow. They soon dried up. Still other seeds fell among thorns and weeds. There was no room for them to grow, so they died after a while. But some seeds fell on good, rich soil. These seeds grew into healthy plants.

After Jesus told this parable, he explained:

- People who learn the Good News but do not accept it are like the path on which the seeds were eaten.

- People who give up on the Good News because it is too hard to follow are like the rocky ground that has little soil.

- People who care too much about owning things are like the soil filled with thorns.

- People who really believe in God's Good News are like the good soil. Faith grows in them. They then share their faith with others.

The Kingdom begins with the Good News of Jesus Christ. It continues when we, his disciples, respond to God's love. We show by our words and actions that God's love is active in our lives and in the world. We pray for the time when God's love will rule the world. We pray for the coming of God's Kingdom in its fullness.

As Catholics...

Saint Elizabeth of Hungary is an example of someone who believed in Jesus and worked to spread God's Kingdom. In the thirteenth century, Elizabeth was a princess in the country of Hungary. She was married and had three children. She lived in a castle and had more things than she would ever need. Yet she spent her life helping those who were sick and poor. She built a hospital and gave food to those who were hungry.

After her husband died, Elizabeth used all of her money to build shelters for those who were homeless, sick, and elderly. Through Elizabeth's words and actions, many people experienced God's love active in the world.

Find out when the Church celebrates the feast day of Saint Elizabeth of Hungary.

parable (p. 252)

🏃 Make up a new parable that describes the Kingdom of God. Use things that are familiar to people today. Share your parable by writing or drawing it. Then act it out.

Jesus' miracles were signs of the Kingdom of God.

Jesus did amazing things that only God could do. He calmed the stormy seas, made the blind to see, walked on water, and even changed water into wine. These amazing events were beyond human power. They were **miracles**.

Jesus' miracles showed that he was divine. They were special signs that God's Kingdom was present in him. His miracles helped people to believe that he was the Son of God.

miracles (p. 252)

 Matthew 14:22–33

One day Jesus' disciples were out in a boat on the sea. Jesus went up to a mountain to pray alone. As night approached "the boat, already a few miles offshore, was being tossed about by the waves, for the wind was against it. During the fourth watch of the night, he came toward them, walking on the sea. When the disciples saw him walking on the sea they were terrified. 'It is a ghost,' they said, and they cried out in fear. At once [Jesus]

Christ Walking on the Water (Armenian miniature, twelfth-thirteenth century)

spoke to them, 'Take courage, it is I; do not be afraid.' Peter said to him in reply, 'Lord, if it is you, command me to come to you on the water.' He said, 'Come.' Peter got out of the boat and began to walk on the water toward Jesus. But when he saw how [strong] the wind was he became frightened; and, beginning to sink, he cried out, 'Lord, save me!' Immediately Jesus stretched out his hand and caught him." (Matthew 14:24–31)

After Jesus and Peter got into the boat the wind stopped. The disciples who were in the boat said, "Truly, you are the Son of God." (Matthew 14:33)

Jesus' walking on water strengthened the faith of his disciples. The first disciples knew Jesus, saw his miracles, and believed.

They told others about Jesus and tried to live as he taught them. By their words and actions, the disciples were witnesses to Jesus.

Witnesses speak and act based upon what they know and believe. We are called to show our faith in Jesus and to be his witnesses.

✖ Write one way you can show others that you have faith in Jesus.

_____

_____

The Kingdom of God grows.

For the past two thousand years, members of the Church have helped one another to be witnesses to Jesus Christ. We can be witnesses by:

- treating people with kindness and respect
- living peacefully with one another
- being fair with all those we meet
- doing what is right even when it is hard
- being faithful members of the Church
- working together for justice and peace.

In the Lord's Prayer we pray for the final coming of God's Kingdom that will take place when Jesus returns in glory. Jesus' coming at the end of time will be a joyful event. It will bring about the fullness of God's Kingdom.

The Church does not pray only for the coming of God's Kingdom. We also ask God the Father to help us to spread the kingdom in our families, schools, and neighborhoods. Everyone in the Church works together so that God's love may be active and present throughout the world.

WE RESPOND

What would you put in a time capsule to show how the Church has spread God's Kingdom? Why?

223

PROJECT

Pray
Learn
Celebrate
Share
Choose
Live

Show What you Know

Write a short paragraph using each of the **Key Words**.

parable

miracles

What Would you do?

Good, rich soil helps things to grow. How can you be the good, rich soil in which God's Kingdom can grow?

DISCIPLE

Reality Check

Your mission as a disciple of Jesus is to help spread the Kingdom of God. Check the ways you can do this.

❏ treat my friends with kindness and respect

❏ live peacefully with family and friends

❏ be fair at work and play

❏ do what is right, even when it is hard

❏ pray in the morning, at meals, in the evening

❏ participate at Mass each week

❏ other _____

Picture This

What do you think you will be doing ten years from today? Draw a picture to show a way you will be living out your discipleship.

Pray Today

Pray the Lord's Prayer. Ask God the Father to help you to work to keep his love alive throughout the world.

Take Home

Jesus told many parables about the Kingdom of God. As a family, read some of these parables found in Matthew 13:33–50. To what did Jesus compare the Kingdom of God?

CHAPTER TEST

Fill in the circle beside the correct answer.

1. A _____ is a short story that has a message.
   ○ miracle   ○ parable

2. The _____ is the power of God's love active in the world.
   ○ Our Father   ○ Kingdom of God

3. In the parable about the farmer who planted seeds, the people who believe in God's Good News are like the _____.
   ○ rocky ground   ○ good soil

4. Jesus' miracles showed that he was _____.
   ○ human   ○ divine

5. Jesus' walking on water _____ the faith of the disciples.
   ○ strengthened   ○ weakened

6. We ask for the fullness of God's Kingdom to come when we pray the _____.
   ○ Hail Mary   ○ Our Father

Complete the sentences.

7. Parables are _____ with a message.

8. A _____ is an amazing event that is beyond human power.

9. Jesus' miracles were _____ of the Kingdom of God.

Answer the following.

10. Write one way you can witness to Jesus Christ today.

_____

_____

"Blessed are those who have not seen and have believed." (John 20:29)

SEASONAL

CHAPTER 27

This chapter celebrates the entire Easter season.

In the Easter season, we celebrate the Resurrection of Jesus.

WE GATHER

Name three things that you believe about God.

WE BELIEVE

Jesus has risen from the dead! During the Easter season, we celebrate the Resurrection of Jesus, for fifty days! We begin the Easter season on Easter Sunday. It ends fifty days later, on Pentecost Sunday.

The color white is a symbol of light and joy. The priest wears white vestments all during the Easter season. The coverings on the altar are white, also. The entire Easter season is a great celebration of the light, life, and joy of the risen Jesus.

Celebrating the fifty days of Easter strengthens our faith. We show our belief in the risen Jesus.

📖 John 20:19–29

On the night of his Resurrection, Jesus' disciples were hiding in a room. The doors were locked. The risen Jesus suddenly appeared and wished them peace.

One of the Apostles, Thomas, was not there that night. The other disciples told him about Jesus. Thomas did not believe them. Thomas wanted to see Jesus for himself. He not only wanted to see Jesus. He wanted to touch Jesus with his own hands!

A week later, the disciples were together again in the locked room. This time Thomas was with them. Suddenly Jesus was there among them. Jesus said to them, "Peace be with you" (John 20:26).

"Then he said to Thomas, 'Put your finger here and see my hands, and bring your hand and put it into my side, and do not be unbelieving, but believe'" (John 20:27).

Thomas fell on his knees before Jesus and said, "My Lord and my God!" (John 20:28)

And Jesus said to him, "Blessed are those who have not seen and have believed" (John 20:29).

EASTER

We believe in Jesus Christ. We believe in his life, Death, and Resurrection. We believe that Jesus brings us new life, now and forever.

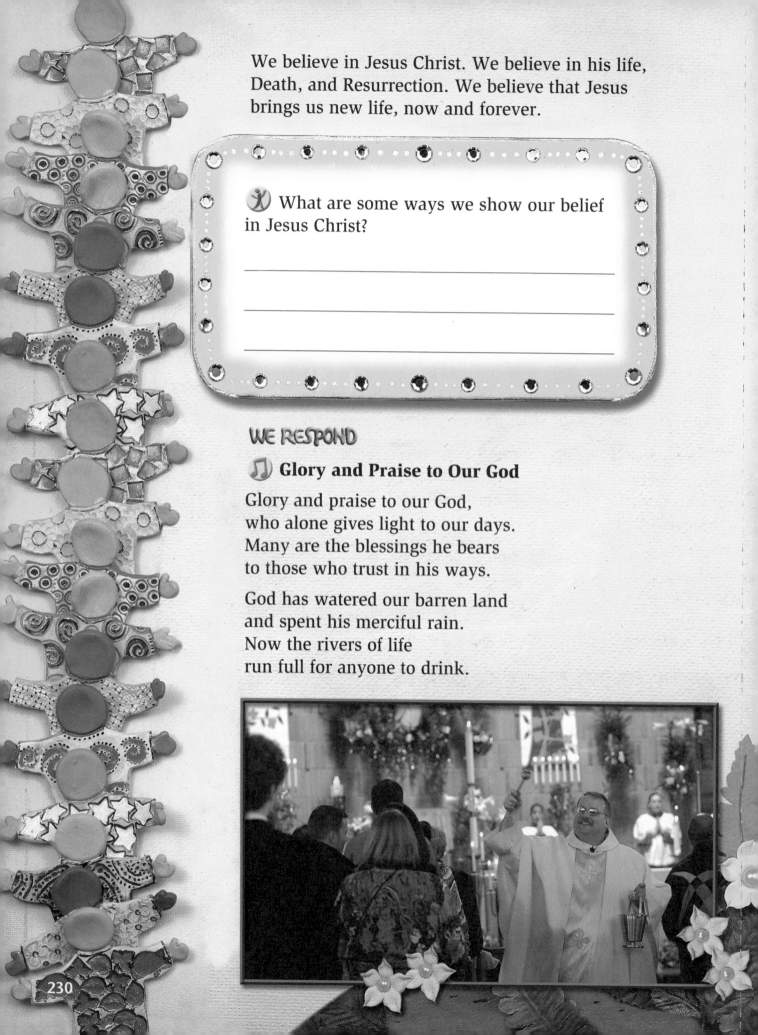

What are some ways we show our belief in Jesus Christ?

_____

_____

_____

WE RESPOND

♫ Glory and Praise to Our God

Glory and praise to our God,
who alone gives light to our days.
Many are the blessings he bears
to those who trust in his ways.

God has watered our barren land
and spent his merciful rain.
Now the rivers of life
run full for anyone to drink.

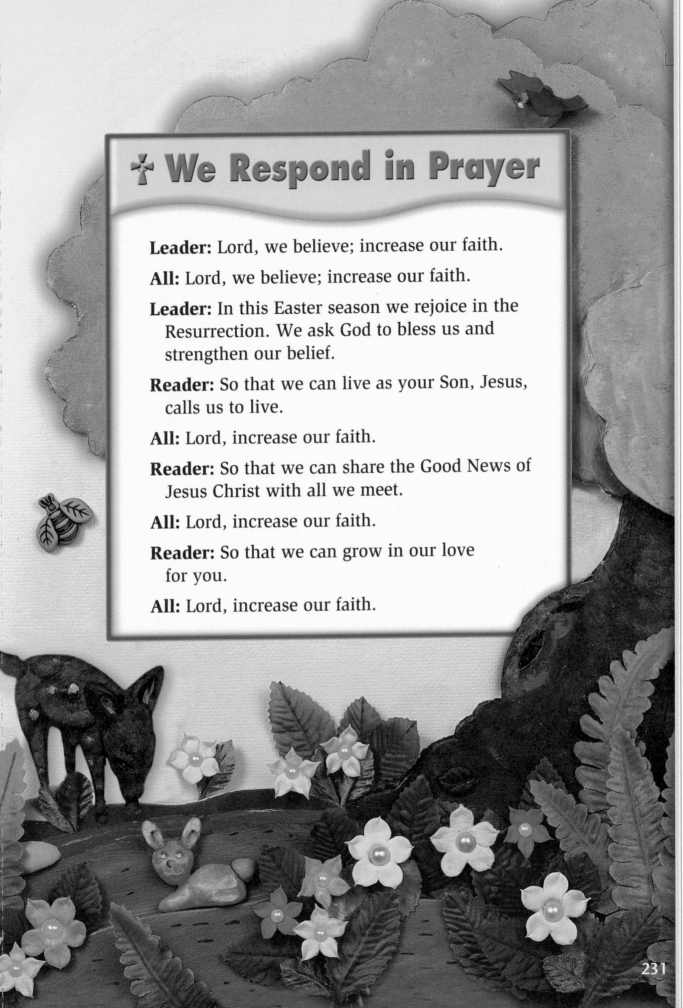

✝ We Respond in Prayer

Leader: Lord, we believe; increase our faith.

All: Lord, we believe; increase our faith.

Leader: In this Easter season we rejoice in the Resurrection. We ask God to bless us and strengthen our belief.

Reader: So that we can live as your Son, Jesus, calls us to live.

All: Lord, increase our faith.

Reader: So that we can share the Good News of Jesus Christ with all we meet.

All: Lord, increase our faith.

Reader: So that we can grow in our love for you.

All: Lord, increase our faith.

PROJECT DISCIPLE

Show What *you* Know

The words in the box are from the story about Thomas. Find and circle the words in the grid. Then retell the story.

B	F	E	T	D	I	P	E	K	G	I	N
L	E	W	C	V	F	A	W	F	A	O	S
E	H	L	Y	A	S	I	C	C	I	P	U
S	L	Q	I	T	E	A	K	T	O	Y	S
S	F	T	E	E	X	P	C	T	N	W	E
E	P	R	B	Z	V	E	P	M	J	E	J
D	U	R	Z	I	R	E	U	P	Q	D	E
A	N	G	Y	R	S	A	M	O	H	T	W
G	U	K	U	I	J	F	D	M	Y	I	L
Z	N	S	D	I	S	C	I	P	L	E	S
R	E	M	X	D	D	M	Y	V	Q	K	C
R	F	L	L	Z	K	E	J	F	F	R	L

believe

peace

Easter

blessed

Resurrection

Thomas

disciples

Jesus

DISCIPLE CHALLENGE Why is this a good story for the Easter season?

_____

_____

 **Pray Today**

Alleluia, Lord Jesus! Thank you for the new life you have given us in the Resurrection.

Take Home

Give each family member a dyed hard boiled egg. Take turns lightly tapping the ends of your eggs together. If one end cracks, try the other end. If both ends crack, you are out of the game. The egg that stays whole or only cracks on one end is the Alleluia egg!

UNIT TEST

Fill in the circle beside the correct answer.

1. Through _____ each of us is called to share the Good News of Jesus.
   - ○ the pope and bishops
   - ○ justice and peace
   - ○ the Sacrament of Baptism

2. Working with other Christians to bring together all baptized people is called _____.
   - ○ ecumenism
   - ○ a mosaic
   - ○ a covenant

3. Catholics who celebrate and pray according to the Eastern Rites and Latin Rite all share in the same _____.
   - ○ sacraments
   - ○ customs
   - ○ languages

4. When we say that Mary was free from Original Sin from the first moment of her life, we are speaking of her _____.
   - ○ Annunciation
   - ○ Assumption
   - ○ Immaculate Conception

5. In a parable Jesus explained that people who care too much about owning things are like _____.
   - ○ the good soil
   - ○ the soil filled with thorns
   - ○ the mustard seed

6. The _____ is the union of the baptized members of the Church on earth with those who are in Heaven and Purgatory.
   - ○ Communion of Saints
   - ○ Assumption
   - ○ Immaculate Conception

continued on next page   233

Write T if the sentence is true. Write F if the sentence is false.

7. _____ A covenant is an agreement between God and his people.

8. _____ A miracle is a short story that uses things from everyday life.

9. _____ When we pray the Rosary, we pray several different prayers.

10. _____ A Rite is a special way that Catholics celebrate and pray to God.

Write sentences to answer the questions.

11. How did John the Baptist prepare the people for the Messiah?

_____

_____

12. What is a saint?

_____

_____

13. What is one way that the Church honors Mary?

_____

_____

14–15. What are two ways we can be witnesses to Jesus Christ?

_____

_____

CONGRATULATIONS ON COMPLETING YOUR YEAR AS A GRADE 3 DISCIPLE!

Fold on this line.

A RECORD OF MY JOURNEY AS A GRADE 3 DISCIPLE

_____
Name

✂ Cut on this line.

Disciples of Jesus share in Jesus' mission.

This year, I shared in Jesus' mission by

_____.

The people who helped me to do this were

_____.

We shared Jesus' mission by

_____.

Disciples of Jesus pray in different ways.

My favorite time to pray is

_____.

My favorite place in which to pray is

_____.

This summer I will pray for

_____

_____.

Disciples of Jesus learn about their faith.

This year, one thing I learned

- about Jesus and the Church

_____.

- about the Kingdom of God

_____.

✂ Cut on this line.

Disciples of Jesus live out their faith.

This summer I will live out my faith

- at home by

_____.

- in my neighborhood by

_____.

- in my parish by

_____.

- visiting other people and places by

_____.

Disciples of Jesus choose to follow the loving example of members of the Church.

This year I learned about Mary and other saints. My favorite saint story is about

_____.

I will try to follow this saint's example by

_____.

This summer I will also follow the loving example of

_____.

Disciples of Jesus celebrate the sacraments.

This year, I celebrated the Sacraments of

_____.

I celebrated with

_____.

Celebrating these sacraments helped me

_____.

PROJECT DISCIPLE

End-of-Year Prayer Service

✝ We Gather in Prayer

Leader: We have learned many things about Jesus and the Church.

Group 1: Jesus sent the Holy Spirit to guide the Church.

Group 2: The Church is the Body of Christ and the People of God.

Group 3: Jesus is with us in the sacraments.

Group 4: Jesus asks his disciples to share his Good News with others.

Reader: Before he returned to his Father in Heaven, Jesus said, "Behold, I am with you always, until the end of the age" (Matthew 28:20).

All: Jesus, thank you for being with us always. May we always do as you ask, sharing the Good News of God's love with everyone we meet.

 Jesus, We Believe in You

Chorus
Jesus, we believe in you;
we believe that you are with us.
Jesus, we believe in you;
we believe that you are here.

We believe that you are present with us here as we gather in your name.
(Chorus)

We believe that you are with us at all times, and your love will guide our way.
(Chorus)

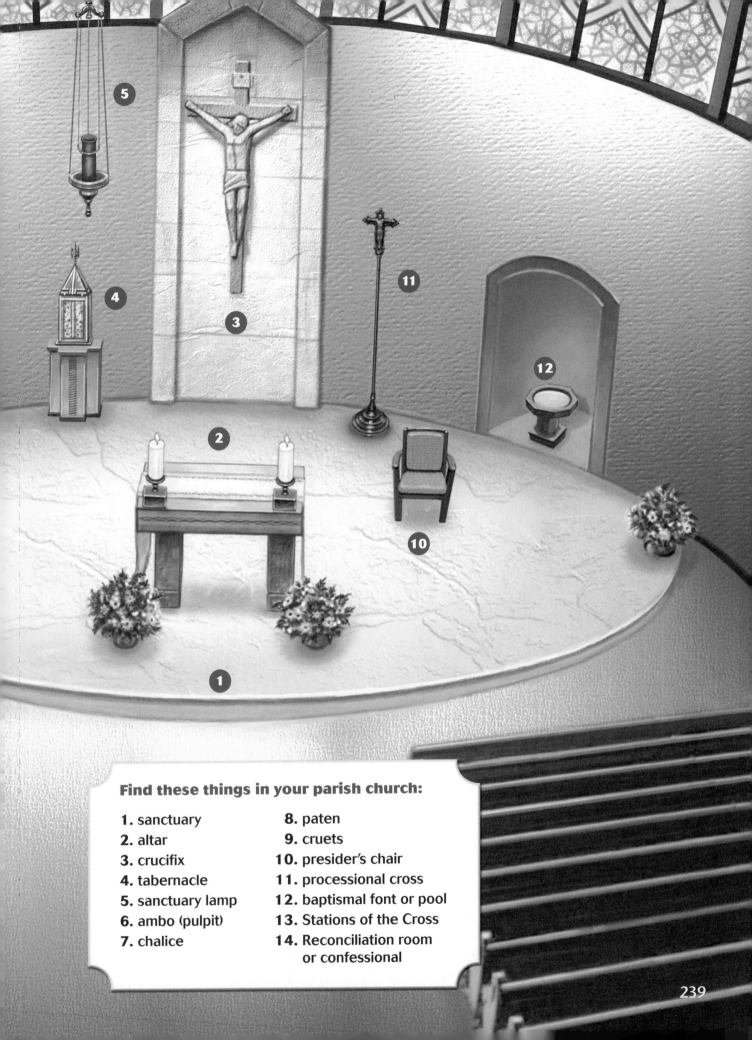

Find these things in your parish church:

1. sanctuary
2. altar
3. crucifix
4. tabernacle
5. sanctuary lamp
6. ambo (pulpit)
7. chalice
8. paten
9. cruets
10. presider's chair
11. processional cross
12. baptismal font or pool
13. Stations of the Cross
14. Reconciliation room or confessional

PROJECT DISCIPLE

You are learning and living out ways to be a disciple of Jesus Christ.

Look what awaits you in:

We Believe Grade 4: God's Law Guides Us.

You will learn about and live out that

- We are growing in Jesus Christ.
- The commandments help us to love God.
- The commandments help us to love others.
- We are called to holiness.

Until next year, pay attention each time you go to Mass. Look around you. Listen.

Here is one thing that I know about God's Law.

_____

_____

Here is one thing that I want to learn more about next year.

_____

_____

_____

We are blessed to have God's Law to guide us!

Prayers and Practices

Sign of the Cross

In the name of the Father, and of the Son, and of the Holy Spirit. Amen.

Our Father

Our Father, who art in heaven,
hallowed be thy name;
thy kingdom come;
thy will be done on earth
   as it is in heaven.
Give us this day our daily bread;
and forgive us our trespasses
as we forgive those
   who trespass against us;
and lead us not into temptation,
but deliver us from evil. Amen.

Glory Be to the Father

Glory be to the Father
and to the Son
and to the Holy Spirit,
as it was in the beginning,
is now, and ever shall be
world without end. Amen.

Hail Mary

Hail Mary, full of grace,
the Lord is with you!
Blessed are you among women,
and blessed is the fruit
   of your womb, Jesus.
Holy Mary, mother of God,
pray for us sinners,
now and at the hour of our death.
Amen.

Find other versions of some of these prayers at **www.webelieveweb.com**

Act of Contrition

My God,
I am sorry for my sins with all my heart.
In choosing to do wrong
and failing to do good,
I have sinned against you
whom I should love above all things.
I firmly intend, with your help,
to do penance,
to sin no more,
and to avoid whatever leads me to sin.
Our Savior Jesus Christ
suffered and died for us.
In his name, my God, have mercy.

• contrition •

• confession •

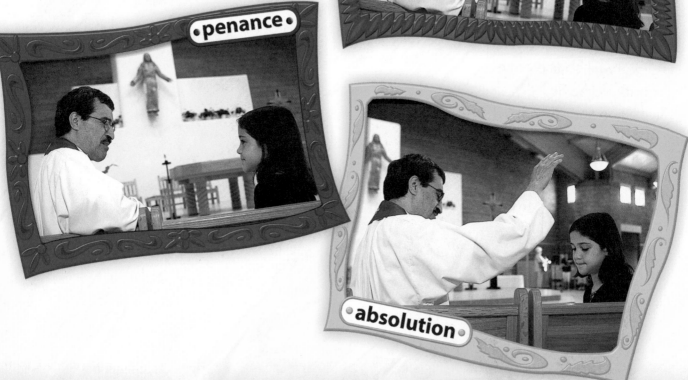

• penance •

• absolution •

Morning Offering

My God, I offer you this day
all that I think and do and say,
uniting it with what was done
on earth, by Jesus Christ, your Son.

Evening Prayer

Dear God, before I sleep
I want to thank you for this day
so full of your kindness and your joy.
I close my eyes to rest
safe in your loving care.

Grace Before Meals

Bless ✝ us, O Lord,
   and these your gifts,
which we are about to receive
   from your goodness.
Through Christ our Lord. Amen.

Grace After Meals

We give you thanks, almighty God,
for these and all your gifts
which we have received through
Christ our Lord. Amen.

Stations of the Cross

In the Stations of the Cross we follow in the footsteps of Jesus during his Passion and Death on the cross.

Jesus is condemned to die.

Jesus takes up his cross.

Jesus falls the first time.

Jesus meets his mother.

Simon helps Jesus carry his cross.

Veronica wipes the face of Jesus.

Jesus falls the second time.

Jesus meets the women of Jerusalem.

Jesus falls the third time.

Jesus is stripped of his garments.

Jesus is nailed to the cross.

Jesus dies on the cross.

Jesus is taken down from the cross.

Jesus is laid in the tomb.

Apostles' Creed

I believe in God, the Father almighty,
   Creator of heaven and earth,

and in Jesus Christ, his only Son,
   our Lord,
who was conceived by the Holy Spirit,
born of the Virgin Mary,
suffered under Pontius Pilate,
was crucified, died and was buried;
he descended into hell;
on the third day he rose again
from the dead;
he ascended into heaven,
and is seated at the right hand
   of God the Father almighty;
from there he will come to judge
   the living and the dead.

I believe in the Holy Spirit,
   the holy catholic Church,
   the communion of saints,
   the forgiveness of sins,
   the resurrection of the body,
   and life everlasting. Amen.

The Rosary

A rosary is made up of groups of beads arranged in a circle. It begins with a cross followed by one large bead and three small ones. The next large bead (just before the medal) begins the first "decade." Each decade consists of one large bead followed by ten smaller beads.

Begin to pray the Rosary with the Sign of the Cross. Recite the Apostles' Creed. Then pray one Our Father, three Hail Marys, and one Glory Be to the Father.

To pray each decade, say an Our Father on the large bead and a Hail Mary on each of the ten smaller beads. Close each decade by praying the Glory Be to the Father. Pray the Hail, Holy Queen as the last prayer of the Rosary.

The mysteries of the Rosary are special events in the lives of Jesus and Mary. As you pray each decade, think of the appropriate Joyful Mystery, Sorrowful Mystery, Glorious Mystery, or Mystery of Light.

The Five Joyful Mysteries

1. The Annunciation
2. The Visitation
3. The Birth of Jesus
4. The Presentation of Jesus in the Temple
5. The Finding of Jesus in the Temple

The Five Sorrowful Mysteries

1. The Agony in the Garden
2. The Scourging at the Pillar
3. The Crowning with Thorns
4. The Carrying of the Cross
5. The Crucifixion and Death of Jesus

The Five Glorious Mysteries

1. The Resurrection
2. The Ascension
3. The Descent of the Holy Spirit upon the Apostles
4. The Assumption of Mary into Heaven
5. The Coronation of Mary as Queen of Heaven

The Five Mysteries of Light

1. Jesus' Baptism in the Jordan
2. The Miracle at the Wedding at Cana
3. Jesus Announces the Kingdom of God
4. The Transfiguration
5. The Institution of the Eucharist

Hail, Holy Queen

Hail, holy Queen, mother of mercy,
hail, our life, our sweetness, and our hope.
To you we cry, the children of Eve;
to you we send up our sighs,
mourning and weeping in this land of exile.
Turn, then, most gracious advocate,
your eyes of mercy toward us;
lead us home at last and show us
the blessed fruit of your womb, Jesus:
O clement, O loving, O sweet Virgin Mary.

Prayer for My Vocation

Dear God,
You have a great and loving plan
for our world and for me.
I wish to share in that plan fully,
faithfully, and joyfully.

Help me to understand what it
is you wish me to do with my life.
Help me to be attentive to the signs
that you give me about preparing for
the future.

And once I have heard and understood
your call, give me the strength
and the grace to follow it
with generosity and love.
Amen.

Holy Water

A holy water font containing blessed
water is placed near the door of the
church. When we enter the church, we put
our fingers into the holy water and then
make the Sign of the Cross. The water
reminds us of our Baptism, and the prayer
we say expresses our belief in the Blessed
Trinity. Many Catholic families also have
holy water in their homes.

Holy Places

We treat places of prayer (churches,
synagogues, temples, and mosques) with
reverence. In our Catholic churches, we
genuflect toward the tabernacle as we
enter our pew. Genuflecting (touching
our right knee to the floor) is a sign of our
reverence for Jesus Christ, who is really
present in the Blessed Sacrament.

Visits to the Blessed Sacrament

Before Mass on Sundays or at other special times, take a few minutes to visit Jesus, present in the Blessed Sacrament. After you have taken your place in church, kneel or sit quietly. Be very still. Talk to Jesus about your needs and your hopes. Thank Jesus for his great love. Remember to pray for your family and your parish, especially anyone who is sick or in need.

Prayer Before the Blessed Sacrament

Jesus,
you are God-with-us,
especially in this sacrament
of the Eucharist.
You love me as I am
and help me grow.

Come and be with me
in all my joys and sorrows.
Help me share your peace and love
with everyone I meet.
I ask in your name. Amen.

The Seven Sacraments

The Sacraments of Christian Initiation
Baptism

Confirmation

Eucharist

The Sacraments of Healing
Penance and Reconciliation

Anointing of the Sick

The Sacraments of Service to Others
Holy Orders

Matrimony

The Ten Commandments

1. I am the LORD your God: you shall not have strange gods before me.

2. You shall not take the name of the LORD your God in vain.

3. Remember to keep holy the LORD's Day.

4. Honor your father and your mother.

5. You shall not kill.

6. You shall not commit adultery.

7. You shall not steal.

8. You shall not bear false witness against your neighbor.

9. You shall not covet your neighbor's wife.

10. You shall not covet your neighbor's goods.

Glossary

Acts of the Apostles (page 52)
book in the Bible that tells the story of the work of the Apostles in the early Church

Apostle (page 23)
one who is sent

Apostles' Creed (page 85)
Christian statement of beliefs based on the teachings of Jesus Christ and the faith of the Apostles

Ascension (page 44)
Jesus' returning to the Father in Heaven

assembly (page 142)
people gathered to worship in the name of Jesus Christ

Assumption (page 213)
the belief that, when Mary's work on earth was done, God brought her body and soul to live forever with the risen Christ

Bible (page 28)
the book in which God's Word is written

bishops (page 77)
the successors of the Apostles who lead the Church

Blessed Trinity (page 20)
the Three Persons in One God: God the Father, God the Son, and God the Holy Spirit

Christians (page 46)
baptized people, followers of Jesus Christ

Church (page 46)
community of people who are baptized and follow Jesus Christ

Communion of Saints (page 212)
the union of the baptized members of the Church on earth with those who are in Heaven and in Purgatory

Concluding Rites (page 151)
the last part of the Mass that remind us to continue praising and serving God each day

conscience (page 158)
God's gift that helps us know right from wrong

covenant (page 197)
an agreement between God and his people

crucified (page 30)
nailed to a cross

deacon (page 101)
a man who is not a priest but has received the Sacrament of Holy Orders and serves the Church by preaching, baptizing, and assisting the bishop and priests

Liturgy of the Eucharist (page 150)
the part of the Mass when the bread and wine become the Body and Blood of Christ, which we receive in Holy Communion

Liturgy of the Word (page 148)
the part of the Mass when we listen and respond to God's Word

marks of the Church (page 78)
four characteristics that describe the Church: the Church is one, holy, catholic, and apostolic.

martyrs (page 54)
people who die for their faith

Mass (page 141)
celebration of the Eucharist

miracles (page 222)
amazing events that are beyond human power

mission (page 44)
special job

oil of the sick (page 165)
holy oil that has been blessed by a bishop for use in the Anointing of the Sick

Original Sin (page 133)
the first sin committed by the first human beings

parable (page 220)
a short story that has a message

parish (page 100)
community of believers who worship and work together

Passover (page 140)
the Jewish feast celebrating freedom from slavery in Egypt

pastor (page 101)
the priest who leads the parish in worship, prayer, and teaching

Pentecost (page 45)
the day the Holy Spirit came upon the Apostles

pilgrimages (page 95)
prayer-journeys to holy places

pope (page 77)
the Bishop of Rome, who leads the whole Catholic Church

prayer (page 92)
listening and talking to God

prophet (page 22)
someone called by God to speak to the people

public ministry (page 22)
Jesus' work among the people

repent (page 22)
to turn away from sin and to ask God for help to live a good life

Resurrection (page 31)
Jesus' being raised from the dead

Rite (page 205)
a special way that Catholics celebrate and pray to God

sacrament (page 132)
special sign given to us by Jesus through which we share in God's life and love

Sacraments of Christian Initiation (page 133)
the Sacraments of Baptism, Confirmation, and Eucharist

sacrifice (page 141)
a gift offered to God by a priest in the name of all the people

saints (page 212)
followers of Christ who lived lives of holiness on earth and now share in eternal life with God in Heaven

second coming (page 37)
Jesus' coming at the end of time

sin (page 156)
a thought, word, or action that is against God's law

synagogue (page 92)
the gathering place where Jewish People pray and learn about God

vocation (page 108)
God's call to serve him in a certain way

vows (page 110)
promises to God

Index

The following is a list of topics that appear in the pupil's text.
Boldface indicates an entire chapter or section.